BORN TO LIVE

THE STORY

Pastor Norman Christie

DEDICATION

For the glory of God, and in thankfulness
for a God-fearing family, who all my life have encouraged
me in the Lord's work.

Endorsements

Norman was brought up in Bethesda Elim Church where his father was the pastor and God's call would also lead Norman into Christian Ministry. It meant leaving a successful professional career with excellent prospects and job security; a major step considering he had a family of three teenage girls and one son. This step of faith would see Norman and Doreen, his faithful and much-loved wife, prove the faithfulness of God time and time again.

His first church appointment was to Randalstown. It was a small church, yet it provided the motivation he needed to see the congregation increase both numerically and spiritually. Believing that God's work requires haste, he immediately committed himself to some building renovations. This decision not only improved the facilities but also enhanced the church's testimony in the town. Numbers increased and there was much excitement amongst members and friends as they enjoyed the blessings of God.

He left Randalstown to return to Belfast and his teaching ministry in South Belfast Elim was greatly appreciated, in particular by the local student population. Other opportunities opened up beyond the local church, and his involvement with the International Correspondence Institute is but one example. Norman was never happier, despite the demanding workload, than when witnessing the spiritual growth of those who had enrolled and graduated in their selected subjects. The achievement of others was his and Doreen's reward. She provided administrative help along with 101 other things. In spite of their busyness, they both experienced the joy of blessedness.

Their next appointment was from one city to another. This time to the City of Lisburn, and Norman would eventually retire from full-time ministry in the Lisburn Elim City Church. However, that was not before experiencing and enjoying much blessing during his time there. A time marked with the completion of a significant building programme. Initially, this was to be a refurbishment and extension of the existing building. However, the project developed into a major building programme, with a new sanctuary, halls, and other ancillary facilities being completed. It is an outstanding complex, adaptable for various uses beyond church services. Significant finances were required which superseded the projected costs, yet today there is a building which is a testimony to God's faithfulness, a place where dreams have become reality and hopes have been realised.

For Norman, the journey from Bethesda, where he sat under his father's ministry, has allowed him, time and time again, to experience God's faithfulness on every hand; this was ever so apparent following Doreen's sudden and unexpected home call.

Doreen ran the race of life seriously and joyfully, never half-heartedly, and she was such a blessing to all who knew her.

I wholeheartedly commend, '*Born to live the Story*' written by a friend, who I have had the privilege of sharing many years of Christian ministry with. His is not the story of a theorist but of a practitioner.

Eric McComb, Retired Superintendent of Elim Churches of Ireland.

It is just over 30 years ago, as a young Christian, I met Norman and Doreen Christie for the first time. I remember with fondness the great sense of love and encouragement I received that evening as I sat in an upper room in South Belfast Elim Church beginning an ICI Course on Christian Ministries. Little did I realise the influence Norman and Doreen would have on my Christian journey, and ultimately on God's call to full-time ministry.

In the 80s – at a time when society was contending with so many challenges, it was an inspiration to find a couple who simply wanted to invest in your life, so that you could be the 'best' for God. Norman and Doreen Christie were that couple. Their sincerity, love, and 'togetherness' in service set the bar of life extremely high for us all – and yet they were prepared to journey with us in order to see us cross that bar! They lived Christ – every day by taking an interest, by praying, through deeds of kindness and encouragement and by setting an example.

Down through the years, I've been both encouraged and blessed to see God's amazing grace manifest in the life of this couple and their family. After the sudden home call of his wife Doreen in 2016, and despite the sense of loss and brokenness and loneliness which sought to occupy his life, Norman held fast to the call of God – knowing that God still had something more for him to do.

After publishing his first book; *A Life Lived With Love* in 2021, Norman continued through writing, to live out and tell the story of his Saviour's amazing love. What you presently are holding in your hand is a copy of a new chapter in the life of a sincere man of God who was, *'Born To Live The Story.'*

Nigel Elliott, Member of Elim Irish Leadership Team, Enniskillen.

I count it a privilege to know Norman Christie as a friend and fellow worker in God's Kingdom. Over the many years of our acquaintance, I have witnessed his growing warm-heartedness, grace and love. His devotion to his Lord and Saviour and his infectious love for God's Word are exemplary. All that he communicates flows out of a genuine, abiding relationship with his Heavenly Father, through Jesus Christ, his Saviour. This very helpful communication includes his first book and his widespread teaching, including his biblical instruction and encouragement of Christian ministers in Zambia.

Pioneers are not always welcomed or appreciated and Norman has been a pioneer, especially in his desire to see the Holy Spirit given His rightful place in the lives of Christians and in the ministry of Christian churches. Like Hannah, he has developed gracious virtues in situations where he was misunderstood. In all that he says or writes, he seeks to be positive and humble, giving glory only to his Saviour. I unreservedly commend Norman Christie to you all.

Pastor Brian Gingles, (co-leader, Barnabas Fellowship of Churches International) B.A. Hons, Dip. Ed. M.A., Larne.

Norman Christie has been a man I have respected for a long time. I first met him briefly as a teenager and he brought wisdom and counsel to my life at that time. Then years later I reconnected with him, getting to know him as a friend and pillar of prayerful support. It has been particularly since Norman's dear wife Doreen passed away that the friendship has deepened.

Norman grew up in a strong Bible-based Christian family, where his father ran a successful business, whilst also involved in part-time pastoring of a Pentecostal church at Landscape Terrace in North Belfast. The rich legacy of a Christian family where gospel preaching and an emphasis on Holy Spirit-led worship, all influenced the young Norman. The memory of a Thompson Chain Reference Bible lying open on a table in the main hallway of the family home has never left Norman. The centrality of Scripture in governing all a church believes and preaches, was not only vital to Norman's father, but to the young Norman, as he grew up in such a blessed family.

Norman went to work as a technician in the Science Department in a Secondary school in North Belfast. Following this, Norman moved to laboratory work in the large BP oil and petroleum refinery which was in Belfast in the 1960s and 1970s but eventually closed. Norman worked there with his Scientific skills and expertise but as time moved on, he felt the call on his life to go out to serve the Lord as a full-time pastor. He became a pastor in the Elim Pentecostal Church and served various churches until his retirement. Following this, Norman preached in a number of mission halls, Elim churches and in other fellowships.

Norman is a very balanced and wise Bible teacher. He blends the best of a Baptist-type of theological emphasis, along with a very conservative Pentecostal experience and belief. This emphasis on Word and Spirit, along with a most generous and encouraging pastoral touch, characterises Norman's approach. A deep interest in Premillennial and Dispensational teaching, influences his approach to Prophetic teaching. Not one to be carried away with extremism or sensationalism, Norman has sought to be governed solely by Scripture in all he does and preaches. He believes God can intervene in lives in mighty power and does all things according to His Providential will.

I highly recommend his story to you. Be encouraged and challenged. A warm heart that conveys a great sense of the reality of God is here for you to follow in the journey he has taken.

Brian Graham, B.Ed, M.A., M.Th., Pastoral Counsellor, Belfast.

Contents

Foreword

Having come from Elim stock but with being a Baptist Pastor for nigh on 40 years, I think the fact that I am writing these few words shows something of the Christian maturity of the man.

I count it a real honour and privilege to be asked to write a brief foreword for Norman Christie's second book.

It was through the auspices of an organisation called, *'Prophetic Seminars'* that we met and our friendship developed.

I have found Norman to be a humble, spiritual brother whose goal in life is to bring glory to his Saviour, the Lord Jesus Christ.

I am sure as you read the following pages, you will be thrilled and challenged as to how the influence of Godly parents and the Word of God being central in family life, has produced this gracious servant of God – a man of prayer.

In perpetuating this family practice, God granted Norman and his late wife Doreen, a family of which he is rightly very proud.

Having endured valley experiences as well as mountain top joys in life, I believe that Norman, having proved God's faithfulness in all things, has become what the Apostle Paul calls, *"a man of God,"* who has followed *"after righteousness, godliness, faith, love, patience, meekness."* 1 Timothy 6:11

Pastor Wesley Crawford, retired Baptist pastor, Dromara.

Introduction

Having observed the positive reactions to my first book, '*A Life Lived with Love*,' I am encouraged to present you with this second offering. The first book contained frank presentations of life and death and my true feelings expressed through poetry seemed to make me almost *too* vulnerable. However, I have since learned that this approach is what the broken-hearted need to receive. As one lady said to me; "*This is real. It is great to know that someone understands.*"

So poignant were the contents of the book that my daughters found it too painful to read. Indeed, such was their love and appreciation for their mother that visiting me alone in my apartment is usually a tearful experience.

I am positively encouraged by people I do not know, especially from the Roman Catholic community; their comments were totally unexpected, but most welcomed.

Having attended as an adolescent, the Technical High School in Belfast, where both Catholic and Protestant pupils were welcomed, I feel more adequately prepared to address our divided communities.

As the reader will observe my humble family life story, I trust that they will feel blessed by the sincere expression of care and respect for everyone.

In many ways this book that you are holding is a testimony of the faithfulness of God in times of adversity and prosperity; His love and faithfulness that He has showered upon all mankind without discrimination.

Jesus invites us to follow His example of faithfulness and unfailing love, while living in a world that is so frequently marred by hatred and strife. In fact, the British way of living was described as a 'dog-eat-dog society,' particularly with regard for children and young people by one renowned international organisation.

Considering the many privileges that we enjoy, what a sad indictment it is!

GK Chesterton, the famous English essay writer, once penned; *"Our children ask for the bread of life and we give them the stones of death."*

Considering the almost epidemic advancement of harmful drugs, these words are tragically still true.

The motto of Belfast is, *"What will we give in exchange for what we have received?"* This echoes the words of Psalms 116:12; *"What shall I render unto the Lord for all His benefits towards me?"*

On a personal note, my name 'Christie' means 'Christ bearer.' The clan motto is 'Thus shall I flourish.'

I pray as you read my story, you will see how I have flourished through Christ my Saviour.

Chapter 1

A Family Business

Both my parents are believed to descend from a French 'Hugenot' background. In accordance with the family name and motto, as shared in my introduction, we rejoice in God's blessing and provision.

Thankfully the Lord has been gracious to us and not only has my family prospered in terms of business but also in discipleship of the Lord. I am a third-generation believer and pastor.

Our family name was also well-known in Northern Ireland for wallpaper and paints.

It all started with my grandfather Richard Christie, known to us as 'Papa,' who was the founder of 'Christie Wallpaper and Paints.' He was originally from a Presbyterian background, growing up in Bethany Church, Agnes Street, Belfast. He was married to 'Ma' as I knew her, who was a very sarcastic woman.

They had three sons, Robert (Bertie) was the eldest, followed by my father Richard and William was the youngest brother. My uncle, Councillor Sir William Christie was born on 1st June 1913. William was Lord Mayor of Belfast from 1972 until 1975 when the 'Troubles' were at their worst.

I recall visiting the Lord Mayor's parlour with my father when I was about 12 years old. His wife was called Selina, she was a remarkable lady who thankfully survived a gunshot wound to her head in 1972. Unfortunately due to his position, his dear wife had become a target for terrorists during the 'Troubles.'

During his term as Lord Mayor in his first year, there were frequent attacks on his business' premises. The *'Christie Wallpaper and Paints'* stores were located throughout the province.

My father in the 1920's was involved in the B-specials. Uncle Willie, as I knew him, was known as a District Inspector (DI) in the B-specials. Due to him living in the North Belfast area which had its fair share of troubles at that time, my father recounted to me that he went to sleep at night with a revolver under his pillow and a rifle under the bed!

Uncle Willie's children were called Noel, Audrey, Leslie and Pearl. It was Willie who developed the company called 'Christie's Wallpaper and Paints Ltd.' The caption back in the early days was; *'No complaints with Christie's paints!'* However in the process of time, it had to be dropped. My father created for him a multi-coloured sign, with each letter of C-H-R-I-S-T-I-E-S being a different colour.

Uncle Bertie had a similar business that was a chain of shops known as 'R. Christie & Company.' So you can imagine, there was a bit of rivalry between them.

My father had his own business also in the same line of work, only he had a team of painters who decorated commercial and residential premises. He was a very successful business man and a pastor. The Bethesda Mission Hall beside the Crumlin Road jail was given to him in 1940. He remained pastor there until the 1990's.

When my father was in his teens, he had fallen for a local girl but things didn't work out between them so he decided to leave in the search for new opportunities. He left Belfast on August 16, 1924, on a boat named Doric, bound for Quebec and then Montreal. He eventually arrived in Ontario, Canada and travelled to a small town called Sarnia and through a meeting with the Salvation Army, he was led to Christ. He later returned to Belfast and after a while, took an interest in another young lady called Hilda Burrows, who was attached to Mateer Street, Salvation Army corps.

Hilda was born in Glasgow in an area referred to as Mary Hill and moved to Belfast as a teenager with her parents, brother and two sisters. Her brother John moved to the States, and became a minister. Bonnie, her younger sister, emigrated to New York, leaving her three sisters, Hilda, Susan and Beatrice behind in Belfast.

Meanwhile a romance sparked between my father and Hilda and they fell in love and got married. They started a family and so my story begins…

Left - Papa' Christie, pictured in 1920, the founder of Christie's Wallpaper and Paints.
Right - Norman pictured with his three older brothers; Leonard, David and Richard.

A baby of the war...

Born in November 1940, at my home in Somerdale Park, Crumlin Road, Belfast, World War II had already begun, so I guess you could say I was a war baby!

I was only six months old when the Germans organised a blitz on Belfast. The country was preparing for a war that would claim many lives. The famous Harland and Wolff shipyard and factories in and around Belfast were needed for the war effort.

Working day and night to make a large contribution towards the Allied response, the people of Northern Ireland rose to the challenge of manufacturing naval ships and aircraft etc.

Initially, the German bombers were targeting the shipyard and the aeroplane manufacturing base in Belfast. My father told me about a British aircraft carrier in Belfast Lough that when the German Bombers came, he said in reference to the aircraft carrier; *"She fired until her guns were red hot!"*

Due to the swift response from the aircraft carrier, the bombers were forced into the city where they dropped their bombs on residential areas. Highly explosive bombs were used in an attempt to decimate Belfast and unfortunately many lives were lost as a result. When the bombing began, as was advised back then, my family hid under the stairs in the house. The cloakroom area was deemed as the safest place to be as previously, in the houses that were destroyed by bombs, it was always noticed that the staircase remained intact in the debris.

So my frightened mother hid with me, her six-month old baby and my three older brothers, Leonard, David and Richard, who were also young children at the time. As we huddled together, my father was standing at the front door of the house watching the planes circle overhead. Obviously, I was too young to be aware of what was going on around me but my brothers often told me later about how scared they were as the deafening roars of the aircraft were heard above our house.

They were targeting a nearby mansion which was completely demolished and later turned out to belong to the German officials. My father continued to watch the planes[1/2] circle above us. He was standing about three feet away from where we were hiding and all of a sudden, they dropped a large bomb! The blast of it flung my father backwards to where we were, inside the cloakroom!

The effect of that explosion had taken my father right off his feet!

Because of the blast, it affected me as a baby and I stopped breathing and started to turn blue. My mother screamed; *"My baby is dead!"*

My father immediately started to pray over me and my breathing returned so I was considered a *'miracle baby.'*

---

1 The **Belfast Blitz** consisted of four German air raids on strategic targets in the city of Belfast in Northern Ireland, in April and May 1941 during World War II, causing high casualties.

2 The **Belfast Blitz** consisted of four German air raids on strategic targets in the city of Belfast in Northern Ireland, in April and May 1941 during World War II, causing high casualties. The first was on the night of 7–8 April 1941, a small attack which probably took place only to test Belfast's defences. The next took place on Easter Tuesday, 15 April 1941. 200 *Luftwaffe* bombers attacked military and manufacturing targets in the city of Belfast. Some 900 people died as a result of the bombing and 1,500 were injured. Highly explosive bombs predominated in this raid. Apart from those in London, this was the greatest loss of life in any night raid during the Blitz. The third raid on Belfast took place over the evening and morning of 4–5 May 1941; 150 were killed. Incendiary bombs predominated in this raid. The fourth and final Belfast raid took place on the following night, 5–6 May. In total over 1,300 houses were demolished, some 5,000 badly damaged, nearly 30,000 slightly damaged while 20,000 required "first aid repairs".

Chapter 2

No wee dolls here

Life was certainly difficult back then due to the environment we were growing up in but I had a stable home and childhood, growing up being taught Christian beliefs and I was well accepted by my big brothers. My mother reported to me later on in life that when I was born, my brother David started dancing and said; *"Good, there will be no wee dolls in this house!"*

Despite being very young, in my memory, the sound of air raid sirens became very familiar and lingers on even until today. Children today play with electronic gadgets whereas back then, we had to make our own fun and even played with the gas masks that we were given. They were readily available as they had been passed out to each family in case the Germans would drop gas on the city.

As the war progressed, I also recall playing quite happily with a drum my parents had bought me, which I used for parades in the street. I used to play it with all of my might! Sadly though, one day a jealous little friend of mine put a screwdriver through the skin of the drum, so I couldn't use it any more. However, my big brothers converted the drum into a cage for a canary bird so it was able to live on.

I also very much enjoyed my American Jeep pedal car. Everywhere I went, my chums would climb on the back for a lift. But one day the axle broke under this pressure, and that was the end of that!

Back then, there was rationing of various foods. My aunt Bonnie, who lived in New York, sent us regular food parcels. I loved helping open the package when it arrived as inside was delicious food, including sugar and other ingredients for making pancakes. She also sent t-shirts, toys and clothes for us. Once I even got a cowboy outfit complete with a gun!

There was an air raid shelter at the end of our street in Somerdale Park. It must have been the only one that had a cowboy nearby!

Unfortunately though, during the war, people were killed in those air-raid shelters, as they were not actually bomb-proof.

Things at that time were dire to say the least! I recall the story my father told us about life during the war. One day as he was walking down our street, some bad news had come through from the Western Front and suddenly, a lady ran out onto the pavement and screamed; *"God has forsaken the world!"*

My father stopped and said; *"Madam, God has not forsaken the world. The world has forsaken God!"*

I recall, I was about seven-years-old when the war ended and I was coming home from school one day, I was amazed to see a huge crane on our street. It's huge iron ball was swinging backwards and forwards, demolishing the air-raid shelter. I was really happy to see it as it had become a smelly eyesore!

At that time there was very little television, and families listened to the news bulletins on the radio. I recall vividly when I was five-years-old, there was a white horse called Snowball. He pulled an Inglis bread cart and frequently came to our door. Seeing the horse-pulled cart full of bread was a very exciting spectacle to me. All of the children in our street loved to see Snowball!

However, sadly, not long afterwards, the horse-drawn vehicles were changed to electric vans.

Playing cricket and rounders with my friends was my favourite thing to do in the street; we would spend hours just playing. But then came the Saturday evening; and we all know what took place on a Saturday evening in a Belfast house – one got bathed for Sunday! But I hated baths. I recall one particular Saturday evening; I was really enjoying the games in the street when my mother called me because it was that dreadful time - bath time.

So once I heard the shout; "Norman bath time!" I promptly ran in the opposite direction!

I ran down the street and crossed the main road without looking at the traffic and I was finally stopped by a policeman! I think he was trying to take my name but he returned me to my parents who were glad to get me home.

I loved looking for newts and fish. As a child, very close to our home was a really black smelling water which had tadpoles and newts in it. Large horses grazed in the middle of the field but quite often, they got caught up in the muddy swamp water. Some were rescued by the fire service who pulled them out using flat hoses. Needless to say everyone was covered in mud! Sadly, some could not be rescued, and they were shot in the head! I remember standing watching from the lane, all of the commotion. After the horse was killed, then shortly afterwards, the butchers would arrive and dispose of the carcass.

I remember one particular day visiting this place and I was straining so hard trying to see the newts, I fell right into it! I went back to the house, dried myself and changed my clothes and went back out again. I almost immediately fell into it again! So I got myself out, went back to the house and changed my clothes. And then, in my third set of clothes, I went down and fell in again and got upset. Whenever I came back to the house, my mother said; *"you have no clothes left, you'll have to go to bed!"*

My mother assisted my father with his work and church pressures and in doing so, got a home help. Our first home help was Mrs Snow. Like some of my father's painters, she was also a Roman Catholic. I recall my mother and Mrs Snow praying together and my mother was convinced that Mrs Snow knew the Lord as her personal Saviour. Following that, she hired Mrs O'Hara who was a Brethren lady and also a believer.

As with most family's coming out of the war, life was quite simple and we had very few luxuries. I recall, during the rationing, when I was five-years-old, we went to Portrush for a holiday. I wanted to go to the beach, to paddle in the sea. Unfortunately, nobody else in the family wanted to go into the water so I decided to go on my own!

The problem was I did not know what to do with my new black boots that I was wearing. Thinking they could be stolen if I left them lying around, I dug a hole in the sand and buried them.

I was having a great time paddling in the sea but when I got back to the beach, I couldn't find my boots. The family came and helped me dig and search, but we never found them. When we went back to the hotel that we were staying in, some of the guests overheard what had happened. They kindly donated some of their rations to help me buy a new pair.

From time to time, we used the Liverpool ferry to travel to the mainland. We were in first class cabins with beautiful oak furniture. As a little boy, I loved the large ship and enjoyed finding our cabin to sleep in. I loved the small blue, red and yellow lights just above my pillow. The result was I failed to get any sleep because of playing with those lights all night.

In 1946, when I was six-years-old, my father purchased our first family car which was a black and chrome Humber Hawk. As he didn't drive, and we were too young, he employed a chauffeur.

In those days' cars could not be driven on and off the ferries. Instead, they were raised with the ship's crane. I remember my family holding their breaths as our car was raised, swung above our heads and then lowered onto the dock.

But don't bless Ralph...

Our street was quite quiet and peaceful, until Ralph arrived!

Ralph was a large vicious Alsatian dog who had just moved into the top of our street. Living behind a locked gate, he snarled and barked at everyone who passed by. We all crossed the street to avoid him. One day however, a nearby friend was walking past with their lovely new Collie pup. Somehow, Ralph managed to grab the pup when he jumped up against the gate.

He pulled the poor wee Collie over the top of his gate, and terrified, the pup just managed to escape his jaws and ran under the family car. Ralph was too large to fit underneath so he continued to bark, snarl and harass the pup. The noise alerted his owners, they tried all manner of things to separate the dogs. And they even broke a spade over the fierce Alsatian's back, before it decided to withdraw sufficiently to get the Collie released from underneath the car. Thankfully the little pup survived and was not injured, just badly shaken. Incidentally, though, he became equally fierce and eventually attacked every dog that passed by the other end of the street. I have often been told that when I was a small child, I was heard saying; *"Bless mummy, bless daddy, (and after listing each member of the family) "But don't bless, Ralph!"*

I had a considerable fondness towards dogs and was delighted as a young boy to get my own little puppy. I visited Smithfield market in Belfast and selected a little high energy pup for only 10 shillings, (50p) I decided to call him Prince and I couldn't wait to take him home so we could play together.

However, upon returning home, Prince turned out to be Princess! She was a mischievous pup who loved gingersnaps! I recall, one day when the laundryman arrived, Prince was on patrol and just as everything was loaded, unbeknown to the driver, she pulled all my clothes back out of the van!

Through time, it was a blessing that I had been mistaken about Prince's gender as she had two litters of pups which brought great comfort to me as a boy.

Chapter 3

Every day is a school day

During the Blitz era, our father moved us to a farm on the side of the Black Mountain belonging to the Fraser household. They treated us very kindly.

I began at Everton public elementary school. Even on my first day, I really wanted to run home, just like the little girl who was sitting beside me!

When I was seven, my father transferred me to another Belfast School, he believed it would be better for me but the standards there were very high. I found it very difficult to adjust. I recall being bullied by my teacher who would grab me by the shoulders of my jacket and swing me around in mid-air. He also would push me from one side of the classroom to the other. (All because I couldn't answer the mental arithmetic questions he asked me to do.)

Furthermore, I was kept in detention after school, not because of misbehaviour, but because I couldn't satisfactorily do the work. After about six months, my health started to fail and my father decided to take me out of the school. After leaving, I contracted Scarlet fever, which was very dangerous in those days.

I slowly recovered, and I then returned to Everton Primary School. I was pleased to be selected as a Centre-forward for our Everton school minor football team. This was a team for boy's under-10-years. Our team turned out to be very successful and we ended up playing for the cup final at the adult Cliftonville football ground. We were very proud as our teacher walked us all out in our lovely blue football strip.

However, the match was a draw, nil-nil resulting in us having the cup for six months and the other team having it for a further six months.

At Everton, I wasn't very bright, but in my report, one of my teachers said that I was excellent at religious instruction. I stayed until the age of 12 when I did my entrance examination to Belfast Technical High School.

When I was accepted, I witnessed all the students achieving their end of year prizes. I determined that I would get something next year. So I worked hard and was promoted into the *'A-stream.'* For the next three years I was *top of the class* and received many awards. However, it was hard for me as I wasn't academically gifted, resulting in migraines due to the pressure I put myself under.

Back then it was very unusual to have integrated education, but this helped me to become more broad-minded. At the school however, teachers didn't always turn up for our Religious Education classes. One day when the teacher didn't turn up yet again, I could almost hear a voice in my head telling me that I should teach the class. It was a frightening idea as there were usually about 60 boys and a couple of prefects in each class! However, a few days later when the incident reoccurred, I bravely stood up in front of everyone and started to talk about the Bible. It was a great privilege to share the Word of God with my fellow classmates, even though it frequently resulted in me being called '*a Bible thumper.*'

I recall one of our teachers throwing our French homeworks up in the air and telling us that we were all going to fail our GCE's!

With the threat of us all failing our GCE's when I got home that day, I was very depressed. I got down on my knees and asked the Lord to speak to me. I started to read from Psalm, 138:6; *"Though the LORD be high, yet hath he respect unto the lowly: but the proud he knoweth afar off. Though I walk in the midst of trouble, thou wilt revive me: thou shalt stretch forth thine hand against the wrath of mine enemies, and thy right hand shall save me. The LORD will perfect that which concerneth me: thy mercy, O LORD, endureth for ever: forsake not the works of thine own hands."*

Reading that Scripture gave me great comfort. I realised that the Lord would perfect those things that were worrying me in school.

When the results arrived weeks later I was the only boy in the school that passed all his examinations. I was most thankful to the Lord for His help and still retain the above promise to this very day.

Once I got to the level of GCE. I was obliged to leave the school, as they didn't do A-levels.

I'm a believer...

I grew up in a Christian home and at 11 years old, I became a Believer. At the age of fourteen, I was filled with the Holy Spirit and was asked to take a Sunday school class. My father was the pastor of Bethesda Church, which was given to him by Albert Osborne in 1940. As such, he invited many godly men into our home. I had the pleasure of playing with my toys while listening to these great men of God. In particular, it was a joy to see the slides about wild animals in the Belgian Congo, which were shown in our home by Mr Teddy Hodgson. Sadly, when the Congo rebellion occurred Mr Hodgson and his fellow missionary Mr Knauf were martyred for the testimony of the Lord. Congo natives have recounted seeing Mr Knauf lifting in worship the stumps of his arms to the Lord as his hands had been hacked off by his attackers.

Their bodies were left to rot on the African soil. Some time later, some native believers were led to recover their bones and miraculously were able to do so despite great dangers.

As I sat at the feet of these legends of the faith, my spirit was stirred within me and I gained a great hunger for the things of the Lord.

At the age of 15, God led me into Sunday school work at our church. I was blessed by the generosity of the senior pastor, Joseph Smith from the Ulster Temple. Pastor Smith, who had become a renowned preacher, travelled to the USA and visited the Assemblies of God circles. While he was there, he acquired an amazing collection of complete all-age Sunday school materials. These products were right at the cutting-edge of Sunday school ministry and I had never seen anything like them in our country.

He gave them all to my father, his close friend and he passed them on to me. The collection consisted of large coloured teaching posters, comprehensive flannelgraphs and amazing teaching materials for each group.

In the process of time, all the teachers had resigned so at the age of 16, I was made responsible for the teaching of all the boys and girls. What a godsend these teaching materials were for a lad who suddenly found himself as a sole teacher of a Sunday school!

Following this, the main Sunday school began to prosper and it became necessary to bring new teachers onboard.

The boys and girls were provided with beautiful take-home pictures and illustrated books for them to fill in. The teaching manuals were crammed with wonderful ideas for creative Bible teaching, which I enthusiastically took on board. What a great help they were for a fresh beginning!

One of the manuals had a beautiful poem inside it called; *'I would Gather Children.'* It was written to inspire teachers, and I still have it in my memory, to this day...

Some would gather money
Along the path of life;
Some would gather roses,
And rest from worldly strife.

But I would gather children
From among the thorns of sin;
I would seek a Golden Curl,
And a freckled, toothless grin.

For Money cannot enter
In that land of endless day;
And roses that are gathered.
Soon will wilt along the way.

But, oh, the laughing children,
As I cross the sunset sea,
And the gates swing wide to heaven
I can take them in with me.

Author Unknown

Chapter 4

A heart after the Lord

One day as I was doing my homework on a Saturday afternoon, the Lord spoke clearly to me and called me into His ministry. At that time, I was listed for two A-levels in the local College of Technology, however my heart was in doing God's work. I started to spend much time in prayer.

Meanwhile, not having been taught Calculus in Secondary school, I was unable to follow the scientific A-levels I was doing. The combined effect was that I failed them and went through a depressed period of unemployment. Eventually I decided to go for the National Certificate in Chemistry and science subjects, and was successful.

During my depressed and unemployment time, my father offered me a partnership in his business, but I declined the offer as I saw a job vacancy in a local Secondary school for a Laboratory technician. I applied, and was successful. Meanwhile, I tried to gain admission to Stranmillis Training College for Teaching but was refused entry.

I applied for a job in the Burnhouse factory outside Lisburn. I was accepted there and my work mostly consisted of performing laboratory tests for foam fire extinguishers.

After a few years, I left there and got a job in the Institute of Clinical Science in the Royal Victoria Hospital, which was in partnership with

Queens University. I was particularly successful and helped a few surgeons with the laboratory testing and research necessary to attain their qualifications. Even though I wasn't qualified in biochemistry, I really enjoyed the work, and was well recognised for doing so. Back then in 1963, despite the salary being only £10 per week, I really enjoyed the laboratory challenges.

A highlight of my youth, when I was seventeen, was when my father took me to the Grand Opera House in Belfast and the International Quartet took part. I will never forget the singing of the renowned Swiss Tenor, Jack Zbinden as he sang the Lord's Prayer. Particularly as he sang; *'Forever and ever, amen.'* I wanted to jump to my feet in celebration but we didn't do that type of thing back then.

Heroes in the Faith...
As I was growing up, I was very excited to hear the preaching of Dr. Billy Graham on the wireless. After much tuning and whistling sounds from the radio, Billy would preach his dynamic sermons on Radio Luxembourg. The programmes were called *'Hour of Decision.'* He became the hero of many Christian boys in Belfast and we all wanted to preach like him. Consequently, many young preachers in the city accidentally developed an American accent overnight, as if they thought it was a signature of success and wanted to be like their hero.

It was in the Summer of 1958, to our great joy, Billy came to Belfast and preached in Windsor Park football stadium to hundreds of people. I had the privilege of organising and training counsellors from Bethesda Church. On the night in question, all of the counsellors got someone to counsel except for me! However, it was wonderful that summer evening to see hundreds of people decide for Christ.

In my early teens, Dr. Jack Shuler held a crusade in the Kings Hall. For me, it was very exciting, thousands of people were packed into the Hall night after night. His dynamic choir leader, Don DeVos had hundreds of singers dressed in white. Many people of all ages turned to Christ. However, I heard the inside story in later years that Dr. Jack Shuler was not at all well. After each service, they rushed him back to his hotel, where a physician was waiting for him, gave him an injection and immediately he retired to bed. This taught me that the calling of God has challenges.

When I was young, I had the privilege of encountering Principal Pastor George Jeffries, founder of the Elim movement. I heard him preach to a packed audience of hundreds of people and as I left the building with my parents, he gave me a warm embrace because of his great love for people, in particular boys and girls.

A few years later, I heard him speak at the then, Wellington Hall, Belfast. He spoke with an eloquent Welsh accent in a soft manner which many folk found easy to listen to. However I recall feeling profoundly sad; this was because this lovely servant of the Lord was no longer being used in preaching the gospel with miraculous signs following.

As a lad in my teens, I spent much time in prayer and bible studies. I recall at the age of fourteen being thrust forward by my mother in a service conducted in Bethesda when the Elim President, Pastor John Dyke was ministering. I recall feeling very small sitting among this row of adults who had all come forward for prayer to be filled by the Holy Spirit.

However, I managed to focus attention on the greatness of the Lord and recall saying such words as '*How Great thou art.*' As the presence of the Lord descended upon us, it dawned upon me that my God was exceedingly great. There were no words that I, as a small boy, could find to describe His Glory. Feeling this burning heat of the Power of God in my chest, I found the Holy Spirit coming to my aid and enabling me to worship God in other tongues. This, of course, gave me the power to witness when the opportunities arose to take Religious Education classes in school. How I thank God for Godly parents who brought me up in the doctrine of Pentecost!

My relationship with my mother was considerably warmer than that of my father. She was of a similar sensitive nature to me, and was always pleased to hear my stories. She was actively involved in my life and she was of a very different character to my father. My father was a bit of a sergeant major. Later in his life, I recall he said to me, *"You probably thought I was hard on you, but I was making soldiers."*

In the book of Proverbs, we are advised to *'train up a child in the way he should go: and when he is old, he will not depart from it.'* Similarly, Proverbs 6:20 teaches us to recall the instructions of our mothers and fathers and apply them to our lives. For example, I recall my father frequently saying; *"If we with unfailing faith, do our part, God will do His."*

Another of his sayings was; *"When it comes to giving, be sure to err on the generous side."*

My father was an excellent teacher of Pentecostal doctrine and theology. When I was mature, he would expect me to speak at the Lord's table, without any warning beforehand. I remember those days with considerable fondness.

I recall as we started to get older, our mother would say; *"It doesn't matter how far you live away from your work, but be sure your home is near the house of the Lord."*

In respect of my brothers, Leonard being the eldest and strongest physically, he was inclined to be emotional and sentimental. He worked hard at the professional side of my father's painting business, and was rewarded accordingly.

When I was still a small boy, Leonard said to our mother; *"Even if I had long trousers and money in my pocket I would never leave you."*

However, when a certain girl called Joyce arrived in his late teens, Leonard was the first to leave! Sadly he is now in a care home in Bangor with moderate dementia.

My brother David was in many ways a contrast to Leonard. He was very proud of his red hair, and in his youth he was frequently involved in physical fights, much to the anxiety of my mother and father.

However, one day when my praying mother was interceding for him, she received a vision of David having his hand raised in the gesture of a preacher. My mother believed what the Lord had shared with her and didn't worry about him anymore. In his late teens, he was converted, filled with the Holy Spirit, and indeed, became a great preacher.

David married Mina but sadly, they didn't have any children.

Richard was of a gentle disposition and grew up close to our parents who referred to him as *'our boy.'* The rest of us were not so well accepted! I recall, when we were young, close to our home was an open well of water. One day Richard fell into the well and was drowning. As he struggled to come up for the third time from the water, Leonard grabbed his thick sandy hair and pulled him right out of the well with it!

Richard grew up and became a leading light in the family business, a worship leader and a pastor of a new Elim church at New Mossley at that time.

He was blessed with his wife Martie and his daughters, Janice, Allison and Vivienne.

Chapter 5

More than a help meet

When I was 18, I was at a birthday party for my friend Sammy. It was there that I met my future wife, Doreen. As the girls all arrived, I saw Doreen and I said, *'that's the girl for me.'* I got to leave her home that day, I was pleased to learn that she lived on the Shankill Road. It wasn't too far from my house but despite the short distance, I even managed to squeeze in a couple of kisses on our way! I recall fondly, each time I kissed her she would say; *"thank you."*

Doreen was born on September 26, 1940, she was a couple of months older than me.

Growing up in Hopeton Street, Shankill Road, she lived with her parents and sister, Alice. Both parents worked hard to provide for their family. The family faithfully attended Albert Street Presbyterian church and Doreen was very heavily involved in the Brownies and Girl Guides.

Doreen was also very interested in children and young people so we were a great match. She was a very warm, loving personable lady and we complemented each other very well. Having committed her life to Christ, at the age of 11, Doreen served the Lord from then to the end of her days. At the celebration of our Golden Wedding anniversary, Doreen was recorded as saying; *"I want to be remembered as the girl who served the Lord to the best of her ability."*

Doreen was bright, cheerful and sociable, bringing sunshine into my life at a time when I was unemployed, frustrated and troubled. We attended the young people's Christian Endeavour, in the Wesleyan Church. These meetings were run by Mr Morrison who encouraged the young people to pray and present bible talks called, 'Topics.'

I recall before Doreen came on the scene, apparently the girls at the church got the impression that I was a very 'religious' boy and wasn't available. So of course, when Doreen and I met, these girls were shocked! They accused her of coming along to the church to get me, so that caused a little trouble. It was not difficult for me to reassure her that my intended friendship was genuine.

Our time at the Christian Endeavour was invaluable preparation for later life, as both our home churches were short of youth. Doreen was gradually introduced to my family at my home church, Bethesda. Being of a winsome disposition, she was accepted by us all.

Doreen was a very busy and productive person. She left Hemsworth School in the Shankill area of Belfast, at age 14. Having inherited an old Singer sewing machine and learning this new skill, when she left school, she began her first job in a clothing warehouse. Whilst attending Singer sewing machine classes, Doreen became sufficiently skilled as a dressmaker to make her own clothes.

When I first met her, she had produced a beautiful lilac dress for the party at my friend Sammy's house. That dress was treasured for many years, and lilac became her favourite colour.

When Doreen reached her 21st birthday, we got her sewing machine electrified and that made things easier for her. Following that, Doreen worked in various shops and then became secretary to a wholesale clothing manager. This gave her experience in working with people and secretarial duties such as typing, which was invaluable preparation for later life.

My relationship with Doreen continued. I recall inviting her to come to our church for the first time, it was a foggy night, I gave her a kiss or two on the way. I had a fairly strict background with three big brothers, so coming into church with a girl was a surprise.

Thankfully, Doreen fitted into our church very well. My mother didn't have any girls, so Doreen became like a daughter to her.

My father accepted her as a Christian girl. When it came to church functions, Doreen got readily involved.

I recall in later years, when my father saw her involved in finance and business around the house. He said to me; *"You are so fortunate to have a girl with a good business head. And that is something you should treasure."*

As far as Doreen's family were concerned they accepted me readily, and showed me every kindness. Although her father had problems with alcohol, he nevertheless worked hard, and I had an excellent relationship with him. As far as they were concerned, I never had an angry word with them on any occasion.

Doreen's mother was extremely hard-working, and couldn't do enough to make me welcome in their home.

While we were dating, we frequently went together on little trips to the Floral Hall at Belfast Zoo and we enjoyed visiting Bangor. As Doreen's family got to know us as a couple, sometimes we were involved in babysitting for their relatives.

Doreen began to teach in Sunday school. Being enthusiastic and compatible we soon got involved in youth meetings in Bethesda and the surrounding area. The church was in a needy area, located at Landscape Terrace beside the Crumlin Road jail in Belfast. It was our privilege to work with deprived children from the Crumlin and Oldpark Road area.

We took annual excursions to Groomsport, increasing from a minibus to a single bus to a double-decker. I remember folk looking on in surprise at the couple of teenagers who organised these trips for the kids and their parents.

Soon we also began the Saturday night youth fellowship. Carrying out these duties while attending the church three times on a Sunday kept us very busy, but they were wonderful days.

I recall in the early days praying to the Lord; *"Father if this is not your will, then break it up!"* Incidentally, I do think some of our young men need to pray that prayer today as I have met some very hurt girls.

Mercifully it pleased the Lord to allow the relationship to grow and I became increasingly confident to continue.

My relationship with Doreen was consistent. We always enjoyed a close relationship. When it came to contemplating engagement, the biggest concern was my need to get a good job, and also the fact that I was young. At that time I was in my early 20's and still working as a laboratory assistant.

Even though I was enjoying my work, when I saw that the BP Oil Refinery was advertising, I noticed that they had much better wages, so I applied and was accepted. I had a period of training before being allocated a role. The wages with BP were good but unfortunately, at the beginning, shift-work was required. I was therefore concerned that my new job was going to interrupt my work for the Lord.

Initially I avoided having to work on a Sunday by exchanging my Saturdays with a friend. This meant that I was able to faithfully carry out Sunday school work and Gospel preaching. Realising however, that my lack of participation on Sundays was causing friction in work, I agreed to do overtime on one particular Sunday when a ship was due to arrive and needed its cargo to be tested before discharge. In the event, the ship was due to arrive at the exact time in which I was required to preach in Bangor. I prayed hard about this matter and was delighted to learn on Sunday afternoon that the boat had been delayed in Wales due to severe fog, which was certainly unexpected in August!

Meanwhile, for Doreen, working in the Co-op grocery store was not the happiest and her mother advised her to change jobs, so she joined a local clothing company. Doreen carried out secretarial duties and looked after their accounts. During this time, we both wanted to get married. There were many conversations about us spending the rest of our lives together. We decided we would get engaged when it was practical to do so.

However, as they say 'time and tide wait for no man.' Since Doreen and I were very much in love and worked well together, one evening before leaving her, I just couldn't contain myself! I made a definite proposal that night in an informal way, and she accepted! That was on November 17, 1962.

Meanwhile, I checked with my father and her father, if that was okay. They thankfully gave us their blessing to continue. We didn't have much money but fortunately for us, one of Doreen's aunts had business relationships with a large jewellery concern in Belfast. The result was, we were able to buy an engagement ring at a wholesale price. So we purchased a four-stone diamond ring, much to the jealousy of others.

Doreen was delighted with it, she really enjoyed showing her new ring to everyone.

During our engagement, I took every opportunity to meet Doreen during the day, as well as in the evening. Sometimes we met at lunchtime and had a romantic walk in the gardens of Alexandra Park. Telephone calls were daily as well.

After two years of engagement, we chose a date for the wedding, August 15, 1964. Doreen's sister Alice and her good friend Maureen were going to be her bridesmaids. Doreen was making the dresses at home.

I recall, when I visited, there was great excitement. As I walked in, all the pieces of cloth were covered, so that I wouldn't know the colour of the bridesmaid's dresses.

Richard, my brother agreed to be my best man, I had been his best man the year before.

Following our engagement, my parents took us both on holiday with them. These were great times of bonding as Doreen was treated as their daughter. In the early days, one of my brothers underlined the difference in the social strata we came from, thinking possibly that I had been taken advantage of. However, years later, he conceded that out of all the boys, I had the privilege of the most happy and loving relationship.

When two become one...

The bible word for a wife is a 'help meet.' That expression is very true as without their help, many men would not have made it, particularly myself!

I was the last to leave home for marriage, my three brothers, Leonard, David and Richard, married in order of age. My mother found it difficult to accept that her last boy was leaving home.

As the wedding approached, Doreen found it increasingly stressful. We had set our eyes upon a little house in the Oldpark area of Belfast.

The houses were in the process of being built. We looked at the plans and loved the prospect of having our very own semi-detached house with a garage.

However, one day my father who wasn't always diplomatic said to me; *"I've got good news for you. Your builder has gone bust!"*

I was really upset and a little angry. I had to share this difficult news with Doreen. Mercifully, we looked around and discovered this little house at 31 Kilcoole Park, North Belfast, which was within our budget, and we both liked it.

It was small, so it would be easy to furnish and it had a garden and a garage. We decided it would be a perfect starter home for us and we were delighted when the sale was agreed.

The wedding day soon arrived. I can remember going out to get my hair cut first thing that morning with Richard, my best man and brother instructing me; *"Get a haircut, without it being too obvious!"*

I remember him also saying to me; *"When you hear the organist playing music to welcome the bride, be sure to steady yourself as it's a very emotional moment."*

My father arranged for an old friend of his, Pastor George Stormont to carry out the wedding ceremony which was held at Bethesda church.

I can still remember standing at the front of the church and waiting for the appearance of Doreen with her non-forgettable radiant smile, which still remains with me.

I could feel the eyes of our 60 guests, looking at me. I was very nervous. Nevertheless, the Presence of the Lord was evident and greatly reassuring, as acknowledged by Pastor Stormont.

I was very happy with the service but some hours afterwards, my eldest brother said he didn't appreciate the minister's humour, for during his sermon he said; *"Norman's the captain, Doreen's the mate and the crew will come at a later date."*

Doreen's minister and his wife attended the service. At the reception, he stated how painful it was to lose one of his good-standing, young people. I can still remember his words at the wedding; *"When I looked around and considered the bride, who can blame him?"*

Top - Norman and Doreen on their joyous wedding day.
Bottom - The Secretary of State speaking to Norman in his role at BP.

The reception was held in the Malone house in Belfast. The meal was good, and the speeches went well. However, I was concerned that we would get delayed but thankfully we were able to get our train on time to take us to Dublin.

That evening, we stayed overnight in Dublin and the next morning we travelled to Dublin Airport. We arranged for our honeymoon to be in St Helier, Jersey, which was very popular in those days. A couple of hours later, we arrived at the St Helier Four Courts hotel. We stayed there for just over a week enjoying the really good weather. We were very happy, but really tired after all the excitement of the wedding.

One of the blessings of my time working for BP was that they gave me an extra week's holiday, because I got married. I was very thankful at the time for a good employer.

We returned home again, via Dublin Airport. At first we thought we would have to stay overnight in Dublin, but thankfully, the flight arrived in good time, allowing us to catch the train home.

Unfortunately, I remember, I didn't get off to a very good start. As I was so anxious to get the train, I ran in front of Doreen not realising I had left her carrying the two cases. So I had to apologise profusely.

We travelled back to our new little home in Kilcoole Park in North Belfast.

For our wedding, my generous father had purchased a Mini car for us costing £530. While Doreen and I were on honeymoon my brother Leonard drove the car around. Back then, we were told that whenever a car reached 500 miles that it had to be serviced.

So, when the time came, I left the car at the local dealership, for its first service. When it was ready, the manager and the apprentice presented the car to me. I said to them; *"If you don't mind, I will just check the oil."* So I lifted out the dipstick and to my surprise, there wasn't even a drop of oil in the car! They had forgotten to pour fresh oil into the engine! I was grateful that I hadn't driven away that day, as the engine of my new car would have seized.

A week or two later, when I had driven the car from the oil refinery in Sydenham to my parents home in North Belfast, I stopped the car and parked it in their driveway. Upon entering the house I shortly afterwards heard a loud BANG! My precious new Mini had decided to go by itself down the drive into the garage door. I ran out in complete panic. I couldn't get into the car, as it was jammed up the side of the house.

Later when Doreen visited, being with a cooler head, she told me to get into the passenger side and start the car up. I did this, and reversed it back.

My parents were away on a Saturday day trip. When they returned home, they didn't notice anything amiss at the end of the driveway.

When they came indoors, I sneaked out and told my brother David that I needed his help. So he came out of the house, and noticed the garage door was all out of shape, so together, we had to try and bang it back into shape!

I recall being on holiday with Doreen and my father and mother in Blackpool. I was required to drive my father's much-treasured Vauxhall Cresta.

However, my father was the worst back-seat driver you could imagine. Unable to drive himself, he sat beside me issuing instructions every mile of our journey. Even though I was an experienced driver, he was acting like a driving instructor and I was the learner. It was very irritating.

The holiday was ruined by his continual interventions, despite the fact that he was paying for nearly all of it. Perhaps he didn't want us to forget, he was the boss!

Chapter 6

Joining the club

The benefits of working for BP were good; they offered a generous payout for families on death, and they paid University fees for children, etc. Incidentally, they also had a social club for the employees. I hadn't joined as my focus was on being at home as much as possible, also, as they started introducing striptease acts, it was not something I wanted to be part of. However, at this time I had started working with Pastor Roy Kerr at Teen Challenge. When the film, '*The Cross and the Switchblade*' was released, I thought it should be shown at the Social Club, which unfortunately meant that I had to join and become a member to gain access. But I decided to do so as it was all in the Lord's work.

So on a particular night, I brought some friends and we played the film and witnessed to the workers as best as we could. Robert Robinson played his accordion and the film was very well received. But meanwhile, some of the workers complained to the management and personnel department. They accused them of a setup, in which they alleged to them that they had deliberately spoiled things by having the film shown, but in reality, the management knew nothing about it and they remained independent.

In due course, I joined with Mr Tommy Green and Mr and Mrs Ronnie Mitchell in training to become Campaigner leaders or 'Chiefs,' as they were known. Our clans were for boys only. Doreen having responsibilities for Brownies and Girl Guides. Quite a number came during the 'Troubles,' from loyalist areas in Belfast. We all became full-fledged Chiefs in 1975.

There were many unforgettable encounters with those rough lads, especially from the Glencairn Estate. However, it was great to teach them the ways of the Lord, and even get them out in uniform for church parades. Fortunately, at a time when the lads started to outgrow Campaigners, Teen Challenge was then introduced to the province by Pastor Roy Kerr. Using the church minibus, these guys were transported to the Teen Challenge centre in Great Victoria Street, Belfast.

The Teen Challenge centre, had been officially opened by the Lord Mayor of Belfast, Alderman John Carson, CBE in 1979.

It was the era of skinheads, glue sniffing and the introduction of drugs and we were right in the thick of it. However, there were also very exciting opportunities to present relevant Teen Challenge 16mm films throughout the province, including both in Protestant and Catholic outlets.

We were granted access to Roman Catholic schools. During the various showings of the film, *'The Cross and the Switchblade,'* many young people in the province yielded their lives to Christ.

On one great occasion, on April 25, 1980, Nicky Cruz came to the Grosvenor Hall in Belfast. Over 100 young people responded to the claims of Christ upon their lives. It was a truly glorious, and unforgettable occasion.

I recall one particular evening involved a very special trip for our boys. We were all at the church having our usual Campaigner craftsmen night when I received an emergency call. Our Teen Challenge projectionists had travelled to Coleraine Elim church with all the necessary equipment, but sadly had forgotten to bring the 16mm film; *'On the road to Armageddon.'*

The church was packed and both the projectionists and the pastor were highly embarrassed. As quickly as possible, we evacuated the boys from our Belfast church, picked up the necessary missing film and headed as fast as we could for Coleraine. The lads were very excited. When we reached the outskirts of the town, the distressed projectionists were standing at the roadside waiting for us. We all hurried into the church, got our teenagers settled and began showing the film. The relief all around was palpable.

After showing this magnificent prophetic film, refreshments were badly needed. To the delight of everyone, we got fish and chips from the shop next door. The lads were now completely hyper, one said to me; *"Can we do this again next week?"*

Who said the Lord's work is not exciting?

I recall, on one occasion, we arranged a special gospel meeting for our younger Campaigners, called *'The Intermediates.'* As usual, I drove the minibus around local streets to collect youngsters but alas it seemed that no one was coming. Beginning to despair, I arrived at the last house in the lower Shankill to pick up the only remaining boy. To my utter amazement, I discovered that this young lad had filled his house with other youngsters in anticipation of the meeting. They all piled in and filled the minibus. Using an expression of speech, I said to him; *"You deserve a medal!"* He took me literally at my word, saying afterwards; *"When can I have my medal?"* Naturally I kept my misunderstood word and I bought him one.

I wonder can we do likewise and take God at His Word? For He is able to do, *'exceedingly, abundantly above all we can ask or think.'*

Through Teen Challenge we did our utmost to promote cross-community evangelism. At that time, one of the political and religious hotspots was in the community at Ardoyne, North Belfast. In those days, there was a small Assembly of God church situated in a very vulnerable position.

We agreed with their pastor, Harry Letson, to show a Teen Challenge gospel film to the local youth.

On the night in question, we arrived at the small church with a minibus full of teenagers from the strongly loyalist Glencairn estate. We seated them at the front of the church and the local, Nationalist lads at the back. The Christian workers were gathered in the middle to stop any possible confrontation between both groups. The meeting progressed peacefully and the Teen Challenge film was presented.

The Catholic lads watched and listened respectfully, but the Loyalists boys were disruptive and mocked the film. When it was all over and the majority had disappeared, seven of the local boys, sincerely returned to hear more about the gospel.

The Lord only knows what was accomplished that evening. Unfortunately, it was our last and only opportunity to go there, because the ensuing 'Troubles' soon reached riot proportions.

Sunnier days...

During the 1970/80's I had the privilege of joining an international teacher/evangelist for outreach ministry in Newcastle, County Down. We had no fewer than seven events each day. At times we stayed in Sunnyholme Caravan Park, where they kindly permitted us to show Billy Graham videos in the reception area.

I was given responsibility to organise the children's Holiday Bible Clubs, which were held on the beach or indoors depending on the weather. Though it was hard work, my own dear wife and young children also greatly benefitted from these events. Each summer over 100 children made decisions for Christ.

These evangelical meetings were held each year during the 'twelfth fortnight' in July. Youth and adult rallies were held indoors and open-air meetings on the promenade in the evening.

Early each morning the large team of workers gathered together for prayer and Bible readings. The training given by our overall leader, (Mr Keith Gerner) was invaluable for the work of the Lord in our respective home churches.

I recall coming home from those special times, only to hear my mother say; "I have never seen Norman's face so lit up with the glory of God."

CHAPTER 7

Feed my sheep

The spiritual fire began to wane a little bit in my late 20's, however the Lord in His loving kindness brought a gentleman into my life, Eddie Moir.

At 29 years of age, this man made a significant spiritual impact upon myself and Doreen. In retrospect, I realise that the Lord was preparing us for ministry in various ways. The Bible tells us; *'Despise not prophesyings'* in Thessalonians 5:20. We therefore received and believed the prophetic ministry of Eddie Moir and were blessed to see it confirmed as truth.

Always of course, we believed in the inerrant Word of God, and as the Scripture teaches us, we learned to accept the prophecies of man with the appropriate scrutiny.

Meanwhile, when still working in the oil refinery, I carried out two crusades in Belfast. The first one was in a converted shop. I can recall speaking night after night after working all day. Obviously, when it came to Friday night, I was very tired. I didn't know what to preach and the place was full. I remember asking the Lord; *"What is happening to me?"*

We started singing; *'How Great is our God,'* and the presence of the Lord filled the atmosphere. Meanwhile, as I stood wondering what I was going to say, an old man at the back prophesied; *"Be sure to listen to the anointed lips of clay and receive the message."*

I was desperate to receive the message myself so I prayed to the Lord.

I had determined to preach at whatever position my Bible opened and it turned out to be the story of Palm Sunday. As I preached, I received more and more inspiration as I went along. I felt so liberated and full of joy, so much so, that I cheerfully wrote the message out afterwards as it was such a blessing to me.

In the early 80s, we had our second Crusade in the City church, Botanic Avenue, Belfast. This in turn relieved me from a lot of internal pressure to become a full-time preacher. Meanwhile I continued working with Teen Challenge. These were certainly challenging times working with such *wild* Loyalist youngsters. I recall one evening standing outside the building on Great Victoria Street, when one of them was throwing stones as a police car was driving past.

I said, *"Son, don't you realise you're ruining your life?"*

He was only 15 years old at the time. And he said to me; *"What life?"* At this time, 'The Troubles' were just beginning in Northern Ireland, but the doors opened to go out and preach the Word. For example, I recall going to a church in Ballyclare, where the leader quoted from John's gospel; *'Ye have not chosen me, but I have chosen you, and ordained you, that ye should go and bring forth fruit.'* Upon returning home, I shared with Doreen that particular verse and that I was quite sure that the Lord was speaking to me.

She replied to me; *"This explains why all day long, I've been receiving visions of all kinds of fruit."*

That is the earliest recollection of the ministry of prophecy and visions which the Lord in His wisdom gave to her. That ministry was to prove invaluable for the rest of my life, and even sometimes took the form of warning me about individuals who would later become untrustworthy.

With Doreen being comparatively uneducated, it was easy for me to see the Lord speaking through her in eloquent measures via visions and revelations.

During this time, my family clearly found it difficult to accept my new role as a freelance lay preacher, ministering in various places and denominations. Their concept was that my brother David was the star preacher; Richard, the worship leader and future pastor while Norman was the Sunday School Superintendent of 28 years.

However the One who said; *"Feed my lambs,"* also said; *"feed my sheep!"* And I felt called to do so.

How important it is, not to try to put people in pigeon holes of our imagination, especially if God is preparing them to do greater things.

I felt I was passed by in the local church. The teachers I had trained in Sunday school were moving beyond me, becoming deacons and pastors.

It was difficult for me, feeling passed over but to be honest, my life was not without its fair share of controversy. I recall, in earlier years when I was involved in outreach to Roman Catholics, it was generally not appreciated. In fact, one day as I stopped to get petrol a leader from one of the churches on the Shankill Road pulled up alongside me, and asked the question; *"Have you denied the faith?"* I thought that was a very harsh judgement. Just because I was involved in cross-community ministry?

Meanwhile, as a volunteer I served among pastors in the Elim Youth committee under the leadership of Pastor Seeman. I had the unusual privilege of serving over the years in three Elim committees. Incidentally, I was never asked to serve in leadership. Again passed over.

One Saturday we brought the youth to Lough Neagh. I was with the first lot of young people who went out on the Maid of Antrim on the water. When we returned to the shore, we prepared the barbecue.

Meanwhile, the remaining ones went out on the boat as we were getting the food ready.

Quite a severe mist come down over the Lough and we could no longer see them.

We became very concerned. But as time went on, suddenly we heard, wafting over the waves, the Hallelujah chorus and we were greatly relieved.

The whole episode reminded me of the fact that on the heavenly shore believers are waiting for the arrival of their loved ones.

As we praise God with our hallelujah songs, they know that we are safe and well.

Sunday school at Bethesda...

At one stage in Bethesda Sunday school, when I was the Superintendent, Elim decided to start a competition for the Sunday school children.

I decided to buy little books for all the children deciding to enter the test. I entered a possible question for each lesson into the notebooks, requesting the teachers to add a further three or four questions for the examination.

On the day of the examination, I checked in with Mr White to see if he had managed to add these further notes for the benefit of his primary class of six-to-eight-year-olds. He replied that he had only used the single questions that I had given for each lesson. Realising that it was too late to remedy the situation, which he clearly misunderstood, we smiled together and I hoped for the best. And that was exactly what happened, of the 10 questions on the exam paper, seven of them I had rightly anticipated for Mr White's class. Therefore, very fortunately they emerged with the best results in the school. Surely another case of '*all things working together for good!*'

We didn't win the competition, but our disadvantaged children did well and the Elim Superintendent, Pastor Sandy Wilson offered his congratulations.

A further interesting but sad episode emerged from my Sunday school teaching days. Back in 1968, I had the privilege of listening to a certain young police constable Arbuckle, as he gave his testimony in our Sunday evening gospel service. I was particularly blessed by his obvious love for the Lord, his sincerity and humility. However, a terrible tragedy arose when within a couple of years; this sincere servant was shot dead in the line of duty.

He was the first policeman to be shot dead by a loyalist on the Shankill Road in Belfast. I later learned that a man from Foyle Street had been arrested in connection with his death.

Because of our Sunday school ministry to many on Foyle Street, I knew the family concerned. Despite being a part-time voluntary Christian worker, through a series of exceptional events, I was granted leave to have an official pastoral visit to see the suspect in the Crumlin Road jail. It was an awesome privilege for me to share the gospel with this man who denied taking part in the shooting. I hoped and prayed that one day he would get right with the Lord.

It would seem that the number of believers killed in the subsequent 'Troubles,' far outweighed their number in society. They of course were ready to go, and were therefore promoted to Glory. Could it be that our merciful Heavenly Father, through their deaths, was speaking to a broken society?

The Sunday school was destined to continue under my leadership until I entered full-time ministry in December 1982. I thank God for faithful Sunday school teachers over the years, such as Mr and Mrs Ronnie Mitchell, my beloved wife Doreen, Mr White, Mrs Mina Christie and others. Among those faithful teachers was a certain Mr Ian Biggart. He was a handsome young man with a winsome personality. Initially, he was appointed as the Bible class teacher. This appointment resulted in the Bible class being very well attended by young ladies!

Some years later, upon my departure in 1982, he replaced me as Sunday school Superintendent in Bethesda.

Chapter 8

When two becomes three

Doreen continued working in the clothing company as a secretary for approximately six months following our marriage and then advised me that she might be pregnant.

We promptly made an appointment at our doctor's surgery on the Shankill Road. As Doreen attended, I waited for her in the car outside. Eventually she returned and joyfully confirmed to me that our first child was on the way.

We were both delighted as we love children and we shared the news straight away with our parents.

Doreen was unfortunately very ill during her pregnancy. Mercifully however, despite Doreen's daily sickness, the doctor didn't put her on the latest medication, which later proved to be dangerous to unborn babies.

Because of my family links with the Salvation Army, it was decided that Doreen would have her first child, at Thorndale House, Belfast. In those days it was very rare for a man to attend the birth of their children, but we kept in touch via telephone.

I recall being informed that the baby and mother were both well and so my joy was complete when I went to visit Doreen as soon as possible.

However, when I arrived I got a shock! I walked in with my guard down, looking forward to seeing my wife. But yet, I quickly learned that things were not all okay.

I was told that Doreen had in fact been in labour for an unheard amount of time. Furthermore, she was very emotional as they couldn't get the afterbirth away, and so they had sent for the flying squad. It was a very emotional moment. I was so shocked, as all I had been told was that mother and baby were well on the telephone. The reality of what Doreen had endured hit me hard. I started to feel really sick. I just about managed to regain my composure and returned to the car without fainting.

Clearly in a state of shock, I drove home very slowly. I was also, however, very thankful that despite all the hazards, Doreen and the baby were reasonably well.

Doreen remained in for one week. I then collected her and the baby and brought them home.

We had a beautiful baby daughter. We named her Sharon.

Unfortunately, Sharon was a poor sleeper. Doreen's mum was a great help to us in those early days. Sharon was very small, getting her to walk was extremely difficult, and she didn't walk until she was 18 months old. All Sharon did before that was bum-shuffle.

We tried rock salt baths and bathing her feet to try and strengthen them. We bought her a toy horse to encourage her to push and walk behind it.

I recall one evening, I was so tired after a long day at work, I eventually got her to sleep. However, just as I got her settled in her Moses basket, I sat down on the sofa and sat on one of Sharon's squeaky toys! Of course, it let a loud squeak out of it and she was wide awake once again! So it was really hard going in those early days and exhausting.

At that time, I realised that the enemy was trying to exhaust us. So we decided to recommit Sharon, to the Lord. That heralded the beginning of better sleeping habits.

We realised we had a very intelligent child on our hands as she started to speak from an early age, repeating every word we said. To encourage her intelligence, I gave her a slide rule, in the hope that she might get mentally tired.

Sharon attended Wheatfield Primary School, where she did really well, and then having passed the entrance exam, went on to the Belfast Royal Academy Grammar School. She loved school and developed a love for children. Sharon was, of course, a daddy's girl.

After doing very well at the Academy, subsequently, Sharon was accepted by Queen's University to study medicine where she got her MB, a few years afterwards, obtaining an MD.

She became a paediatrician at the Children's Hospital in the Royal Victoria Hospital, Belfast. Having studied microbiology as part of her preparation, she was quickly promoted to consultant specialising in infectious diseases.

Meanwhile Sharon was happily married to Dr David Sharpe on September 21, 1995. Their two mature children, Rebekah and Katherine have been actively involved for years in church outreach ministry at home and overseas. Sharon is now very heavily involved in hospital activities, including the further education of doctors in respect of the care of children.

"The crew will come at a later date..."

As was mentioned at our wedding, our family started to expand. When Sharon was only a couple of years old, on November 24, 1967, Hilary was born. What a wonderful surprise she was!

I recall on the day she was born, the doctor left Doreen just before lunch and said; *"You have a while to go!"* But against the doctor's expectations, Hilary arrived at lunchtime.

Hilary was small, but was a better sleeper than Sharon had been. She was a very happy child. Hilary really enjoyed nursery school and loved to entertain everyone with her songs and rhymes.

The sisters got on very well together, and they loved playing with their dolls. We continued to be well supported by both sets of parents.

Hilary was bright and attended the same schools as Sharon, demonstrating a real love for the school and indicated very early on that she wanted to become a school teacher. It therefore came as no surprise when she came out with a First-Class Honours degree in Religious Education.

Hilary applied for a job in a local Primary school. I can remember driving her to the interview, and as we reflected on her life she said to me; *"I've really no chance of getting a job here, because our family has a history of working in concrete jungles!"*

However, in fact Hilary was immediately accepted, and they clearly thought that she would be very useful in the school's future. Being a pastor's daughter, she was very compassionate and excellent in the pastoral care of needy children. Hilary can tell you many moving and wonderful stories and she frequently receives many gifts and is very grateful for this. Today she is now the head teacher in her school. This school has over 600 pupils, which is very large for a primary school in Northern Ireland. During the recent outbreak of COVID-19, they had to remain open to teach vulnerable children, and for essential workers children, which equated to 200 boys and girls.

Hilary is now married to Pastor Roy Johnson, who is Elim's Irish Missions director.

When Hilary was three years old, Pamela was born on July 22, 1971. She was a little redhead, the strongest of the girls and was bursting with energy.

She used to say; "Press the button!" Then she would charge through the house at top speed!

Pamela also attended grammar school, but was not as academically inclined as her older sisters. Pamela went to Richmond Grammar School. However with moving to Randalstown it interrupted her education, and she had to attend Ballymena Academy. Pamela inherited her mother's ability at financial and business activities, spending some years in a local building society as a supervisor.

When the opportunity arose she became finance officer for the Elim International Missions. In other words, she started working for her brother-in-law Roy!

On July 2, 1975, our only son, Philip was born.

In school, Philip thought the teachers knew nothing! He was a typical rebellious boy. Philip, unlike the girls, wouldn't work in school; his reports were dreadful. It was only when we bought him a Commodore computer, we discovered he was gifted in that way. While others went to university and learned about computers, Philip took them apart and put them together again to see how they worked!

However, the following incident indicates that the Lord loved him, and was interested in him. I recall on one occasion, he told his mother that he couldn't do his exams, because he had broken his thumb.

She marched him upstairs and was really angry. She went up to his room to give him a piece of her mind, but when she walked into his room she saw a vision of angels, which had a calming effect on her.

Philip attended Antrim High School and he was reasonably happy there. Unfortunately we had to transfer him from there to Belfast, when we moved.

He was successfully employed by firms in Northern Ireland. Then he applied to a large International company, who cheerfully accepted him and he rose through their ranks passing and helping various members of staff who were highly qualified. He is now very professional within his industry. He keeps his highly educated sisters right as he has become a pro with computers! Philip rejoices in having two young children.

Chapter 9

Early married life

Doreen was a housewife, raising Sharon and Hilary in our home in Kilcoole Park, and we then moved to Abbeydale Crescent in North Belfast, where the remaining children were born and grew up.

During these years, I remained working for BP. The children were blessed with great Christmas parties organised by the oil refinery, and were given substantial gifts. After a while, when they discovered I was involved in kids' work, they gave me an active part in organising these parties.

Meanwhile, Doreen was still managing the Brownies and Guides in the church with considerable success. Our own girls benefited greatly from these organisations. We learned that one of the best ways of keeping families together was for parents to participate in organisations which involve their own children.

My oldest daughter, Sharon vividly remembers the night of her first Girl Guide display at age 11. A couple of weeks earlier, her younger sister, Hilary had chickenpox. As she got ready for the display in the old Bethesda church, Sharon discovered that she had the chickenpox rash. She said to Mum; *"I've got chickenpox!"* Doreen being the Girl Guide leader said; *"Cover yourself up. Don't worry about it. The show must go on!"* Sharon had an important part in the play, and seemed to be indispensable.

I was still working with the young boys in the Campaigners; one of the badges they were encouraged to do was the collector's badge. I recall one of the loyalist boys told me that he had collected bits and pieces from the army shops and had wanted to bring his collection that day in order to get a badge. I loaded all his memorabilia into the boot of my car. When we reached the church, I was unpacking the boot when I noticed an army patrol was at the top of the street. Quickly thinking, I invited the soldiers into the church to see the collection, and they all took it in good heart. I breathed a sigh of relief!

On another night at the Campaigners, there was an attempt to steal my car at the front door of the church. It had an automatic locking device on the steering wheel, because of which, the thieves only got it moved across the street. Once again the army arrived and suspected there was a bomb inside it. Thankfully we were able to discuss the matter and stop them from blowing it up. The car boot was empty!

During the 'Troubles,' at the Ardoyne Roman Catholic chapel, there were two armoured vehicles parked across the road, creating a checkpoint. Just as we approached them, an IRA sniper opened up with an automatic weapon at the checkpoint. The people in front of us were bundled into an armoured vehicle. I asked the soldiers; "*Could I do a U turn?*" They agreed, so I turned quickly and drove back as fast as I could!

Meanwhile, in our home at Abbeydale Crescent, I was awakened during the night, by the sound of gunfire. I could hear the bullets whooshing over the top of our bungalow. My immediate concern was for my wife and children. I knelt at the side of the bed, and prayed earnestly; "*Heavenly Father, please don't let them wake up!*" And the Lord was gracious, and they slept through it all. The shooting lasted for about an hour.

The next day I learned that a gang of IRA men had climbed on top of a nearby school, and were firing their weapons in an effort to terrorise the estate. My neighbours phoned for help, advising the Security Forces that we were all under attack, but nobody came.

Incidentally, from then on, the army didn't get their usual cups of tea! Following their rampage, the IRA men targeted Ligoniel industrial estate where they opened fire on the Royal Marines, who were on guard duty. They fired back and one IRA man was killed, and another injured.

Meanwhile, we continued to be very busy with the Lord's work. Doreen was excellent at home finances and organised all the grants for the university etc. She was a wonderful wife. Doreen got a job at Ballysillan nursery school as a cook about 12 years after we married.

She also applied for a job in administration, at Stranmillis Training college, and was successful and enjoyed a happy few years there. I found myself being very busy working for BP and looking after my family.

Meanwhile I was involved in teaching and preaching in various areas around the province. I went quite often to a place situated in the infamous murder triangle called Five Mile Hill. The meetings there were run by the late Sinclair Halliday; he had converted a pig house into a mission hall which was located six miles from Newry.

One Sunday I was driving to a particular evening service there and the car suddenly lost most of its power, leaving me driving about 15 miles per hour. I eventually arrived in the yard having decided to carry on.

As the service continued, his sons looked at my car.

While I was inside I could see a picture on the wall. It said; *"'Tis grace has brought me safe thus far. And grace will lead me home."*

So I took great comfort from that sign on the wall, and I believed that the Lord had indeed brought me this far, and the Lord would get me home. So we stayed on and enjoyed a late supper together, leaving the farm about 10:30pm that Sunday night. Unfortunately though, I had only driven about a mile, when the car started to lose power again.

I was determined to make it onto the motorway to get some help, but I couldn't get the car to go above 15 miles per hour. So I pulled onto the hard shoulder as I was a hazard to others. Then this car pulled up in front of me, observed Doreen wearing a hat, assumed we were religious so offered to tow us.

He asked; "Where are you going?"

I replied; "We are going to North Belfast, to Abbeydale Crescent." To my amazement, he told me he was also going to North Belfast but to Abbeydale Drive! It turned out he was a Brethren preacher returning home on his way from Enniskillen.

It was very stressful that evening as we had the children in the back, especially during the 'Troubles,' it was quite scary to have a car broken down. So with flashing lights, I was towed down the motorway with Doreen and the kids in his car. We got to Belfast without incident and we disconnected the tow rope. Slowly I drove home and eventually parked my car in the garage, being extremely grateful to the Lord.

My friend brought me to work the next day and when my car was looked at, it was discovered there wasn't even a drop of petrol left in it! However even in the darkest days of the troubles, there were times of humour and laughter. I recall the need to purchase a wheelbarrow to help with the old jobs around the garden. I drove with Doreen into Belfast City Centre, hoping to get one from a large department store.

However, we ran into difficulties when it proved impossible to get close to the store because the 'Peace line' was blocking the way with large concrete blocks and soldiers on guard duty. However, Doreen being the keen shopper she always was, headed off to the large shop, while I remained in the car.

In those days vehicles that were left empty were blown up by the army, and Doreen couldn't drive so I had to watch as she disappeared down the blocked street. Shortly afterwards, Doreen returned wheeling the wheelbarrow, through the concrete blocks to the accompaniment of the soldiers singing; *"And she wheeled her wheelbarrow through the streets."* If I needed evidence of my wife's love and care, it was plain to be seen that day.

I cheerfully add that though there were stressful events in those days, the constant reassurance of my wife's loving support was daily a great source of inspiration.

Furthermore, at times when I was at wit's end corner, the gracious Holy Spirit granted her a prophetic ministry, which gratefully lifted my shattered spirits.

The Bible's description of a good wife being 'a help meet' was vividly true, for in every way, Doreen helped meet my needs of the hour. We give God the glory for how he integrates into our lives and works for the advancement of His Kingdom.

Doreen still enjoyed dressmaking and during the early childhood of our three daughters, Doreen made all their dresses and in turn when they got married, she made all the bridesmaid dresses for their weddings, just as she had in 1964 for our own wedding.

In later years, our eldest daughter Sharon asked Doreen to make the bridesmaids dresses for a neighbour's daughter, who was about to get married. The daughter attended University in Cambridge, and Doreen at first, reluctantly agreed to make the dresses.

The dresses were greatly appreciated and so we were invited to Cambridge for the wedding.

Doreen really enjoyed that trip because she always loved to be amongst students, possibly because she had been denied the opportunity to be one herself.

For Cambridge, we had to travel to London first and we found ourselves having to navigate our way around the London Underground. When we stopped to change at the station, there were no lifts, so we had to climb the stairs carrying our cases. We managed to reach the first landing, then I left Doreen there and climbed up to the street level carrying two cases, to check where we were. In the midst of the very busy crowd emerged a young black gentleman who was already carrying his own two cases. Seeing Doreen's predicament on the landing, he put her case under his arm and cheerfully climbed upstairs, carrying all three cases.

How remarkable it is that in every nation, there are strangers who are willing to help! In the midst of a heaving throng of people, such help was badly needed and most unexpected.

Chapter 10

Stepping into full-time ministry

Sadly at that time, the BP oil refinery was no longer profitable and in the early 80's it closed down, making all the workers redundant including myself.

It was a depressing time for all of us who lost our jobs but I took it as an opportunity to serve the Lord in a full-time capacity.

When I told Doreen that I had lost my job, and was now looking forward to full-time service, she was ready to, *"crown me with the frying pan!"* However, grace and love prevailed and she readily accepted having to adjust to various types of employment, and supported me wholeheartedly in my new dubious career.

Having been brought up in the Elim church and enjoying several years of preaching throughout the province, I applied to the Elim church for a full-time position and was accepted. I was made a probationary pastor at the age of 42. However, I was required to carry out certain academic studies and face exams at degree standard.

In December 1982, I was offered the opportunity to pastor Randalstown Elim church, a smaller gathering that had been struggling to stay open.

When we arrived, the congregation doubled overnight with the arrival of our family. Prior to this, the only members were six older ladies. They were very pleased to see us! Meanwhile, Elim H.Q gave us a measure of financial support.

Thankfully, through time, the work in Randalstown prospered and the congregation started to grow. It was certainly a time of great transition for my young family but I was well supported by Doreen. I recall one of my colleagues in similar pastoral trials saying; "*I reckon pastors' wives are a special kind of breed.*"

Despite us having to deal with numerous problems and difficulties, one of my critics in Randalstown managed to say; "*Doreen is a girl in a million!*"

Inevitably, such were the pressures of having girls at university, a humble salary, and a small congregation, my redundancy money got used up and a bank overdraft occurred. I received word that the bank manager required me for an interview. As we had always done, we presented our needs in prayer to the Lord. We needed a few thousand pounds.

Within 24 hours, prayer was answered, the overdraft cleared, and a bank official embarrassed, because we had been called in.

As I got used to my new role, the church started to grow. Friday night became the family night service; people came from various churches to these meetings. On these evenings, we invited along fine musicians such as Pastor Bill Dunn and other popular singers at that time. On those nights, people often enjoyed 16mm gospel films and cups of tea.

We had the joy of seeing a number of people coming to the Lord, including a young Presbyterian lad who later grew up to do outstanding work in Africa. On one occasion we went to a special meeting celebrating his efforts for the Lord in Kenya. Clearly the local ministers did not realise that there was a Pentecostal pastor among the congregation for at one stage one of the ministers said; "*I thank*

God that I am not one of those happy clappy empty-headed charismatics!"
Naturally, I did not respond.

On one occasion at our Friday night meetings, we had a visit from an
International singer, called 'HoneyTree.' I was told by her agent prior
to the visit that she normally received about £500 for each appearance.

I informed him that we could not raise such an amount of money but
I would cheerfully give all the money we received that night from our
offering. The agent agreed and we proceeded to advertise the arrival of
'HoneyTree' to the church. Unfortunately, the advert for her coming was
placed among the concerts etc. in the local newspaper. Just beside our
advert there was a picture of a scantily-clad musical group appearing in
the area. When one old lady saw this picture beside the church advert,
she immediately reacted angrily and assumed that I was bringing such
persons to the church. However, when the evening came, 'Honey Tree'
thankfully arrived very modestly dressed and the old lady concerned
realised her mistake.

Just before the service that evening, I drove the minibus around the
area to pick up those who wanted to come. Meanwhile, 'HoneyTree'
was trying to set up satisfactory sound arrangements but I was away,
and there was no one to help. My 10-year-old son Philip came to the
rescue and adjusted the controls of the sound equipment. 'HoneyTree'
was delighted with the fact that she now had perfect sound.

Sadly, we didn't have a particularly large crowd in attendance but
'HoneyTree' turned out to be a wonderful musician and singer with
a delightful personality. She certainly knew how to woo people
and entertain the children. Philip was enormously proud when she
introduced him as; *"this little guy who came forward to help and gave
me perfect sound!"*

For an International singer to say such kind remarks was truly flattering
for my little son.

In those early days in Randalstown, every effort was made to attract as many folk as possible to this sadly depleted church. In particular, Gospel Crusades were conducted by Evangelists George Wallace and Dan McVicar. Indeed my elder brother Pastor David Christie conducted a Gospel Crusade from September 16-30, 1984, Sharon Reid, Raymond Crookes, 'Arrival', 'Salt' and others provided music and songs.

In addition, with excellent help from my family and friends, Holiday Bible Clubs were organised for the children and proved to be very successful. Doreen headed up the Ladies' Fellowship and organised rallies which filled the church to capacity.

We were very grateful to Second Randalstown Presbyterian Church, who kindly loaned their church hall to us for Christmas dinners etc. Life was tough for my family in Randalstown, even after we eventually moved into the area. However, one of the lasting blessings from that fellowship was the commencement of the ICI College of Ulster. We subsequently brought this ministry to Belfast when we were asked to pastor South Belfast Elim church. The ICI College of Ulster became widespread throughout the province.

I shall always be grateful to Randalstown Elim Church through which I was soon ordained in the Ulster Temple as an Elim minister. I am happy to say that the congregation during our stay was sufficiently enlarged for other pastors to take over. I was then asked to go to South Belfast Elim church.

CHAPTER 11

South Belfast Elim

Having been called to South Belfast, problems arose concerning the purchase of another home and the resettlement of my family. House prices in Belfast were considerably higher than those in Randalstown.

Having shared with the church leadership the probability of buying a new house at Four Winds, we were eventually relieved of the stress of both finance and the strain of commuting from Randalstown.

For some members of the family, the move involved making decisions and changes which were stressful. I particularly regretted having to move my son Philip from his secondary school in Antrim where he was happy and making progress.

Having secured a home in the Four Winds area, the family settled very happily.

I was particularly glad to return to the city and get involved with the local people in a sharply divided community. The church was situated in a political 'hotspot' where paramilitaries from both sides lived in close proximity.

The immediate Protestant community beside the church had very good relationships with the members of the congregation. The result was that frequently I was asked to visit and conduct funeral services for people whom I didn't necessarily know. I remember one old lady saying to her friend; *"Be sure to ask the pastor to bury you, for he does a lovely wee service!"*

I recall a notable occasion when members of both the IRA and the UVF were gathered in the church for the funeral of Mrs McBurney. This exceptional lady, being the mother of one of our Elim pastors, had initially been brought up in a Roman Catholic family; hence the reason for the diversity of interest! To begin with, the atmosphere in the service was really tense but as we showed our appreciation of the lady concerned, everyone seemed to relax.

As he was leaving the church, one Catholic gentleman shook my hand and said; *"You were quite right Pastor, to suggest that Mrs McBurney was in heaven because she was christened in our chapel!!"*

During our stay at South Belfast Elim church, the IRA exploded a bomb near the local police station in Donegal Pass. We surveyed the damage in the local area and were thankful that the church suffered only minor damage to the roof. Whilst standing near one of the severely-damaged houses, we were most fortunate when a large slate tumbled down from three storeys up and smashed on the ground at the feet of myself and my youth worker. We were so grateful to the Lord for His protection and indeed, that protection was witnessed on other occasions.

One such time was the annual Donegall Pass Festival. The controlling committee had arranged for a number of amusements to be active in the area such as swings, roundabouts etc. I was sitting in the church office when an emergency telephone call arrived, it was from the local Brethren church in Apsley Street. They informed me that the police had arrived and advised the amusement workers from the south of Ireland that it was not safe for them to stay in the area because the UVF were active nearby. Some of the workers had already withdrawn their caravans and equipment from the site. I rushed around to them and I was met by a group of frightened southerners who were about to leave. In good faith, I assured them that they would come to no harm, while inwardly, asking the Lord to protect them. They accepted my assurances and bravely stayed on the site. Consequently, the children and youth in the area had a wonderful time and the workers enjoyed gospel films etc. In the mercy and faithfulness of God, I am delighted to write that neither the workers nor equipment suffered any harm.

Meanwhile, Gospel services were also held in the nearby Shaftesbury Square, at the lunchtime outreach. So things were very busy indeed.

However, it was not all fun and games. The church also promoted educational, Christian courses from the International Correspondence Institute. (ICI) These were largely at a college or degree level standard, requiring an external written examination. Such courses were recognised by the Elim Bible College (EBC) and it was possible through them to claim an exemption from the EBC's preliminary study year. These courses would eventually lead to a BA degree, awarded by the ICI.

Locally, students studied not only the individual courses but attained the ICI certificates; Church Ministry Certificate, The Christian Message Certificate and The Christian Counsellor Series.

Between January 1987 and February 1993, 388 men and 54 ladies from approximately 37 churches and 10 denominations were taught.

In addition, parallel studies were held in the Ulster Temple; Ballyclare, Maghera and Larne Elim churches.

ICI courses were also held at intermediate and basic levels in various centres. Since it was not possible for everyone to go to Bible college, these courses were invaluable to married people and part-timers. One of the deeply satisfying outcomes of it all is that subsequently, a number of our students became full-time pastors.

Following the closure of the ICI college of Ulster in 1996, two students continued their correspondence courses with the ICI and were granted BA degrees.

Also during this time, my daughter Sharon qualified as a doctor with her MD degree in 1989, Hilary qualified with her B.ed of Education, First-Class Honours in 1990.

For all these educational blessings, both in the ICI and family life, we give God all the glory.

Special moments...
Doreen and I celebrated our 25th Wedding Anniversary in 1989 at South Belfast Elim church. To celebrate, we were blessed with a wonderful holiday in Austria, thanks to the generosity of our daughter Sharon.

It was a very exciting time as also that year, Dr Billy Graham came to the UK for 'Mission '89.' There were live-link relays from the 26th June to the 1st July in various UK venues, including Belfast, all relayed live from London. We joined with other churches in the area, in prayerful preparation of training and committee meetings.

The live-link consisted of a large screen in The Crescent, a local Brethren church which portrayed what was happening in London. During those local meetings, which were very well-attended, some 15 people responded for counselling. All of them were in fact, seeking assurance of salvation. I discovered upon counselling an older lady who was clearly a believer, that her dad had never told her that he loved her. She said he was very kind but she couldn't remember him ever saying he loved her.

Realising that she had projected this lack of affirmation upon her Heavenly Father, I was able to correct her insecure thinking. I have since discovered that this kind of problem is common among people who lack assurance of salvation.

Now, I wish to place on record the unwavering devotion and loyalty of my family as we served God both in Randalstown and South Belfast Elim. Doreen was always a tower of strength in visitation with me and prayerful preparation for the meetings. Inevitably, Doreen would lead the women's work and carefully prepared all manner of activities to help the local ladies. Her close walk with the Lord resulted in many folk being helped because of her prophetic gifts, visions and revelations.

People loved to hear her as she preached on Mother's Day, some other occasions and in Nursing Home's etc. Her frank talks about family life were frequent sources of comfort and amusement to the listeners, quite often at my expense!

When it came to catering for special events, she excelled in bringing much joy to a lot of people. However, it was as the mother and matriarch of our family circle that her example of love, work, devotion and protection, will never be forgotten. In every way, she served the Lord gladly to the best of her ability and that is the way she wanted to be remembered.

Many recognised her as an ideal pastor's wife, who's loving compassion for all was a great example. Frequently, many visiting speakers and missionaries would reside in our home and be blessed by her cheerful attendance and catering. In particular, she loved entertaining children from the '*African Children's Choir.*' I praise God for such a wonderful wife and co-worker and rejoice in the time He gave us together.

From an early age, we sent all our children for music lessons, believing that it would help them grow in their development for life and the Lord's work. What a wise and necessary decision that proved to be!

Thank God all of our children got saved and upon entering the Lord's work full-time, the musical contribution of each one was invaluable.

Sharon played both the organ and the piano, Hilary excelled with Pamela on the piano and singing while Philip enjoyed the drums. All got involved in Sunday School teaching and youth work. How gracious the Lord has been to us all!

Through our ICI classes, Hilary became acquainted with a certain trainee pastor, Roy Johnston. What a wonderful and lasting relationship this has proved to be! They were married in South Belfast Elim on July 15, 1991. Both ourselves, Mr and Mrs Sydney Johnston and our families were all present for the joyous occasion.

A further beautiful, though sad story emerges from our stay in Belfast.

I was invited by a young man called Brian to visit him and his widowed mother in Sandy Row. Upon arrival in their humble home, I learned that Brian, who had a degree, suffered a dreadful physical attack in the city centre and was rendered an invalid thereafter. As part of the conversation, he said that he wanted to donate something to the church in his will. I thanked him but secretly thought that this poor guy could at best leave us a TV and a suit. How far from the truth! Later on at the time of his death, he informed me that he had a rich uncle in Hawaii and thanks to this uncle's generosity and Brian's kindness, the church benefited to the receipt of over £100,000.

We were blessed with the privilege of representing absent parents when many of our Malaysian Chinese students graduated from Queen's University. It was also wonderful to conduct their wedding ceremonies, and the dedication of their children.

The wedding of Dr Ho and his bride, Mei Ying was an unforgettable experience. Their parents travelled from Malaysia for the event, and beautiful Malaysian flowers were flown in to decorate the occasion.

The local community were all invited to the reception in the church youth hall, where both Chinese and Irish food was available. The presence of the Lord was wonderful and the singing of the Chinese choir really inspiring.

In South Belfast Elim, our Chinese students mostly came from Malaysia, however one student came from Hong Kong and her father was a restaurant owner. She wanted to be married in the church so we set about organising her special day.

When the day came, the bridal party arrived about an hour and a half late for the service, whereupon the best man decided to immediately take photos. The bride was dressed in a beautiful, very expensive-looking white dress covered in pearls, whereas her mother arrived in her everyday clothes and slippers.

After the service, the wedding reception was held in the Europa Hotel where one floor was taken over by the restaurateur and his chefs preparing everything. I recall the first-course was Shark fin soup. My wife and I were treated as honoured guests at the top table and found ourselves surrounded by bottles of alcohol, which seemed to be the best money could buy. Since we were both tee-totallers, it was of no benefit to us but I am sure the guests enjoyed themselves with all the liquor and a dragon dance afterwards. We left early that evening as I needed to teach an ICI class afterwards.

One unforgettable occasion occurred when the International Chinese Heavenly Melody Singers arrived to take part in an Elim Belfast crusade in the Ulster Hall. I accompanied them for lunch in a city centre restaurant. As we queued up in the restaurant, I introduced them to the counter staff. One staff member said; *'Would they sing for us?'*

They agreed and sitting at their large table they began to sing; *'Guide me O thou great Jehovah.'*

The whole restaurant remained silent as in beautiful harmonious tones they sang; *'Bread of heaven, feed me till I want no more.'*

It was truly a remarkable lunch hour, and everyone was blessed by it.

In South Belfast Elim church, we had some excellent members, whose ministry influenced the local people. Mr Davy Hughes, who now lives in the USA, was a church elder. He was full of compassion, and did much to help the local people, raise funds for the church, and preached in the open-airs and in various mission halls. His daily work as a porter in the Royal Victoria Hospital, brought him into contact with many needy people, who required prayer and counselling. The truth is, he was more of a pastor in the Royal Victoria Hospital than a porter!

Mrs Kathleen Moore was a superb Sunday school superintendent, rendering much help to vulnerable children. Her husband, Mr Alan Moore, looked after the church finances very well, especially in those days of financial constraints, when we were still paying off the church mortgage.

James Thompson was installed as an assistant minister in the autumn of 1991. He arrived with his wife Julie and their two children, Aaron aged 3 and a half and their new baby Jonathan. Despite having happy relationships with James and his wife, one Sunday in the early days, I noticed that Julie was clearly upset. Understanding her close relationship with her dad and former pastor, Tommy McGuicken, I quietly said to her; *"You are missing your dad, aren't you?"* Fighting back a few tears she replied in the affirmative. However, they stayed in South Belfast and even continued after I had been sent to Lisburn Elim in 1993.

Frequently, there are family stresses in pastoral church life, which congregations may not understand.

Chapter 12

"Fear thou not; for I am with thee."

While still serving the South Belfast area, I was invited to pastor Lisburn Elim church. I was concerned at this request as I had been informed that the church was badly split. However, the leadership believed that a new pastor seemed necessary to give everyone a fresh start. I prayed earnestly to the Lord regarding this move but I still didn't receive an answer each time when I prayed about going. I believe this happened because I was afraid. However, upon confessing my fears to the Lord, I received immediate guidance to take up the post. In 1993, I arrived in Lisburn and was installed in the church.

It certainly wasn't an easy task, the church leadership had all resigned and feelings were running very high. I spent much time in prayer, calling out to the Lord for His guidance as I knew only He could direct my paths. At that time, I felt comforted by Isaiah 41:10; *'Fear thou not; for I am with thee: be not dismayed; for I am thy God: I will strengthen thee; yea, I will help thee; yea, I will uphold thee with the right hand of my righteousness.'*

As I spent much time deliberating over how to move forward with the situation, I realised that the deacons would have to be reinstalled as soon as possible in order for each entity to be represented. I set about contacting everyone involved but unfortunately on the night when the deacons were due to be reinstalled, there was a problem. I received a phone call from one of the proposed deacons, stating that he was not going to appear because he had another engagement. I reacted strongly and told him that he ought to make an appearance and that before the meeting, I would arrange for him to be reconciled to another deacon, with whom he had issues. Thankfully he agreed and I gathered both men in the office. Whenever the service outside started, I said to them; *"Gentlemen, you have to forgive and forget and make a fresh start in your relationships this evening. I will shortly be taking you outside. In front of the congregation you will be required to shake hands together with all the new deacons. You have to do this because the whole congregation is watching, and the groups who are represented by these various deacons need to publicly see that reconciliation at the leadership level has commenced."*

They reluctantly agreed, and we joined the congregation outside for the consecration of deacons.

The result was that the church was saved from being further split, but sadly the enforced reconciliation brought about tensions, which continued to the very end of my pastorate.

My initial fears were, as you will appreciate, well founded, but in the mercy of God, I enjoyed my time in Lisburn Elim Church and I was kept there for 18 years.

During this time I continued my roles on various Elim committees, such as the Youth Committee, the ACE committee and to this day, the Pastoral Care Committee.

After about one year, we sold our house in Belfast and set up our new home in the Highfields area of Lisburn. In the early days it was necessary to enlarge the church's repertoire of songs and choruses. My daughter Pamela and her boyfriend Kyle, who still remained in South Belfast Elim, did a great job in enhancing the songs of Lisburn Elim.

The arrival of Pastor Roy Johnston and his talented wife, Hilary was a great source of blessing. After a comparatively short time, he was promoted to Associate Pastor, on March 31, 1996. Their contribution to the pastoral care of our youth and children was immense.

With the Elim church beginning in Monaghan in 1915, we were privileged to celebrate the 75 years of Elim in Northern Ireland in 1990. The 'Special celebrate 75' series of meetings were held in Lisburn Elim in 1996. Speakers included Pastor Eric McComb, Pastor Roy Johnston and myself. What a great time of blessing that proved to be!

It was a very eventful year, but not without it's sadness for we were obliged by reasons beyond our control, to shut down the work of ICI.

This was particularly shattering for both Roy and myself, who with great efforts had advanced and lectured in the school on a voluntary basis. However we pressed ahead with our dynamic programme, seeking only the glory of God and salvation of precious souls. Our grief was further compounded by the internal, unnecessary complaints and criticisms.

Unfortunately, 1996 became known to us pastor's as *'the year of rejection.'* However, souls continued to be saved, and bodies healed.

Despite all the conflict, which was destined to continue for years, we also received a number of thank you letters and cards, which are retained until this day.

What strength, we derive from God's Word!

2 Corinthians 5:9 says; *'Wherefore we labour that whether present or absent we might be accepted of him.'*

However, there were also lighter moments. We began a meeting for the *'singles and young marrieds.'* One young man wanted his older friend to attend these meetings; "For after all," he said; "They were married young too!"

We were to be blessed by the ministry of Pastor Alec Tee from Scotland over several years, resulting in the salvation of souls and the healing of the sick. The teaching ministry of pastor Ralph Sykes, from the USA was also greatly appreciated. I recall this gentleman of God praying for the sick. On one particular occasion and totally unexpected, as he prayed for this lady she fell backwards, with considerable force. At that moment, I was only gently supporting her but the impact was so severe that much to my embarrassment, I also was lifted off my feet! Thankfully, neither of us suffered any injury!

Among our special guests was Pastor Ron Jones from Wales. Pastor Jones, though around 80 years of age, ministered in the fellowship very effectively over a period of several years. He was most certainly anointed by the Holy Spirit and at times he was accompanied by a Welsh tenor singer.

We also had the privilege in those early days of welcoming visitors from the mission field, such as the Buxton's, evangelist David Greenow, a singing group from Belarus, Jose Pedro Filho; president of the Elim churches in Brazil, not to omit a fine local Bible teacher, Pastor John Harris.

At this time, the late Mr Ian Biggart and his wife, Ena, joined the fellowship, following the closure of Bethesda due to 'The Troubles.'

Ian was in charge of the TV studios at Stranmillis teacher training college. He soon struck a warm friendship with Pastor Ron Jones who frequently broadcast on the Vision Channel, which was a Christian TV channel operating from Swindon. Special permission was granted for the video recordings in Stranmillis. When there were free slots, Pastor Ron made several recordings there under Ian's supervision. Excellent professional master tapes were produced from the small studio for Swindon. These included, 'The Roberta Clements Story,' 'The wonders of God's love,' (for four studies) and interviews with local leaders such as Pastor James McConnell and Pastor Bob McMullan, etc.

In 1997, a special series of united interdenominational meetings were held in Lisburn C.W.U, entitled '*Lisburn Arise.*' Video recordings of those special gospel meetings were also made.

The video recordings of the meetings of Lisburn Elim began to be made every Sunday. Mr Tom Tate then produced CDs from these videos which were greatly appreciated by those who were not able to physically attend church. Not to mention, grateful families when special events such as weddings and baptismal services were recorded, giving them a memorable keepsake.

Thinking of Mr Tom Tate, we gladly remember his faithful service over the years with the Lifeline youth club. I also appointed him as Church treasurer in 1993, which work he diligently carried out until 2012. His many skills developed as a former maintenance manager in the local prison were also invaluable in church day-to-day business.

Meanwhile in 1996, the church choir began under the leadership of my daughter, Hilary. In addition, Hilary was greatly anointed in leading the praise and worship team.

As far as possible, we planned to cover the needs of every age group. This included family ministry, in particular, Pastor Roy Kerr of '*Family Life Foundation,*' who ran a special series of meetings.

However, like all the families of God's people, we were saddened from time to time by the deaths of beloved friends.

High on that list was our beloved caretaker, Mr Tommy Mateer. What a devastating blow was his sudden death to his wife, Sadie and family members! He was greatly loved by both myself and Pastor Roy. We were grieved by his unexpected departure to glory, while we remembered that he was, *'with Christ, which is far better.'*

Nothing was too much trouble for Tommy, who was working for the Lord on the very day that he suddenly collapsed in the street and died instantly, which was September 24, 1998. Tommy's undying loyalty to the Lord, his family, his country and the local church will never be forgotten.

Standing in the musical gap...

Now, among the frequent visitors to Northern Ireland during the 'Troubles' were the Tharp family from the USA. They travelled all over the country, living in their large bus, which was well-equipped for the purpose. They had a much-needed ministry for both sides of our sadly divided community. Their ministry to both Catholic and Protestant schools was amazing. We had the privilege of the Tharp's and their team coming on several occasions to our church in Lisburn, where they ministered the Word with music and songs.

I recall sitting in the Waterfront Hall in Belfast City Centre, listening to boys and girls from Catholic and Protestant schools in Ulster bringing their tributes to Marty, Sharon, and the team. It seemed that the good Lord said to me; *"Here is a man who is willing to stand in the gap."*

Certainly, I myself have from the beginning of our friendship known him to be *that* kind of man.

Even in local church life, I recall prior to one of our advertised Church Harvest services, when the proposed musical band took ill, Marty, Sharon and their team didn't hesitate to help and gladly took their places.

In Ballee High School at the beginning around 1980, or St. Louise's around 2002, they were teaching our kids to love God and love each other.

They stood, also in the musical gap, cleverly adapting worldly songs to sacred themes. They attracted our youths with such numbers as, *'Jesus can heal your Achy Breaky Heart.'*

Similarly they stood in the spiritual or religious divide by praying for all our people, ministering to both priest and pastor, Roman Catholics and Protestants. They were still ministering in Ulster in 2010, when I was about to retire from full-time ministry.

In those days, the ministry of the church was greatly enhanced by Hilary's ability to produce dramatic productions. These productions were very useful in her school and also in church life. One of Hilary's outstanding plays was entitled, *'Resurrection Reality.'* It was a presentation of a court scene in which various people were dressed up as court officials. The case was then argued between the barristers and witnesses concerning the resurrection of the Lord Jesus, or otherwise. This play was very well presented and many folk attended and enjoyed the proceedings.

Every year Pastor Roy presented a special mission for boys and girls in the month of August. Sometimes dressed up as Bonio the clown, he presented such interesting programmes as *'The Heroes,'* encouraging children to stand up for the Lord Jesus and become a hero for Him.

Meanwhile, we were delighted to prepare young couples for their weddings. The preparatory classes and the wedding ceremonies were sources of great joy. Doreen in particular enjoyed the excuse to buy a new outfit, which of course, always had to be from a sale, to make it affordable.

In particular, I remember the marriage of Roy and Margaret, who both suffered from severe health conditions. Like two wounded soldiers, they were destined to lean heavily upon each other. In becoming Mr and Mrs Roy Crothers, they established a happy and faithful relationship. They were also one of a few couples who benefited from Doreen's excellent catering, as with her ladies, she prepared their wedding reception in the church hall. The hall was suitably decorated for the joyous occasion.

However, I have to add that sadly Roy lived only for a few further years, leaving Margaret to be a widow.

Chapter 13

Dealing with the highs and lows

As can be clearly seen, the life of a pastor is very much a roller-coaster experience. I recall attending a conference for Elim pastors, where I had occasion to speak to a trainee pastor, who was also accompanied by a senior minister. I said to the trainee; *"Please remember that in this work, the highs are very high, and the lows are very low."* Immediately the senior minister interjected and said; *"Words of wisdom there, don't forget them! And unfortunately, I have to tell you that there are more lows, than there are highs!"*

I thank God for the opportunity I had to encourage a young man called Steve Mitchell, who had a great vision for reaching boys and girls.

He established the organisation called the *'Primary Vision,'* and I had the privilege of being one of the members of his advisory board. He was heavily involved in school morning assemblies and he conducted up to 20 Religious Education classes every week. The entire teaching programme was based on the R.E curriculum for Northern Ireland, which meant that teachers also worked alongside with what he was doing. He was also able to share in Scripture Union and Christian Union groups at lunchtime, and after school hours. In addition, he took family services at the weekend in church settings. He enjoyed the privilege of leading holiday club programmes for boys and girls, particularly during the summer months. The work was further enhanced by Sunday School teacher programmes and all this ministry was done as a faith programme. It depended entirely upon the Lord and His people for practical support.

I recall when I was working on a part-time basis at Teen Challenge on Great Victoria Street, Dr. Brock, a Christian psychologist came over from the USA to help train us. His area of training for us was counselling, including personality profiling.

Dr. Brock told us this story which was very helpful to me.

In his studio, he was asked to see this lady who was in deep mourning. She travelled across the States to see him, dressed in black with her son. Her other son had died of cancer. She was all in black, even had a black flower.

When he spoke to her, he found there were two or three problems wrong in her thinking. So Dr. Brock said to her; *"When your terminally ill son told you he was dying, how did you react to that?"*

She replied; *"I told him it was nonsense, he was not dying, God would heal him."*

She said; *"Every day I told him he was going to live but he didn't."*

So then Dr. Brock understood her condition more perfectly. He said to her; *"Do you not realise that you were causing your dying son considerable pain? Because the Lord had shown him he was going to be taken home but you wouldn't accept it. Clearly you were angry with God. And your sinful resentment is stopping you from recovering from the loss of your son."*

He continued; *"Can you imagine that you are in that room where your son is lying in the coffin?"*

She replied; *"I can clearly see my son lying in the coffin."*

He said; *"You need to in your mind, go over to that coffin and apologise to your dead son for not accepting that God was calling him home."*

She went through the motions and did that.

Then he said to her; *"Don't you realise that you sinned against the Lord by not accepting His revealed will, so you will need to pray and ask for His forgiveness."*

After doing this, immediately her expression changed. She even managed to smile.

The sorrow of losing her son was undoubtedly dreadful but the wound could not be healed because of her resentment.

It could be likened to yellow pus in a physical wound, the resentment needed to be dealt with. So then in front of Dr. Brock's eyes, she began to recover because it had been dealt with.

She returned home and made a normal recovery from the devastating loss of her son.

Clearly Dr. Brock was teaching us that there were two emotions working with this lady, resentment and mourning.

For me, it was a lesson I would never forget.

Not so long ago in Lisburn, Pastor Roy Johnson and myself were called to pray for a church leader who was terminally ill with cancer. As I sat in the car outside the home waiting for Roy, my son-in-law to come. I opened my Bible and over and over again, I was directed to scriptures about heaven and home.

We were greeted at the door by the man's wife, who was clearly an outstanding believer. Upon coming into the living room, I met my old friend, church leader and his daughter, though from a different denomination. He said, holding back the tears; *"We recognise you as a man of God and so we sent for you in our desperation."*

His wife then said; *"We have a promise box and I have been taking promises from the box, which indicate healing and life."*

I found myself in a very difficult situation, as I knew in fact, my old friend was dying.

I clearly couldn't contradict her, especially in front of her husband. So I said, with the emphasis on the *'if;'* *"If* God has spoken to you, you must accept what He says."

We prayed gently that the Lord in His mercy, would restore this suffering servant. This was done for the sake of the loved ones. But in our hearts, we knew he would be restored and healed in heaven.

In a few weeks he had passed away.

This true story illustrates for me that promise boxes only speak positive things.

When we consult the Bible, we get both the negative and the positive. There is after all a divine appointment *'once to die.'*

The lost of the lost...

In obedience to the Great Commission, it has been my privilege to preach the gospel in many and various settings. One of the most challenging areas to present the gospel was in the loyalist 'Tiger Bay' area. As the opportunities arose it has been my privilege to address the congregation of the 'Jesus Saves' church in the Tiger Bay area for the last several years.

Accompanied by my close friend, John Wylie, the gospel musician and singer, we have enjoyed many happy visits to that fellowship. I greatly admire the evangelical zeal of their minister Eric Smyth, former Lord Mayor of Belfast. Under his leadership the congregation have demonstrated great zeal in distributing tracts and the Word of God in their area and throughout the city. Despite their difficulties they remain faithful to this day.

It was most interesting to read an article in one of our notable national newspapers, 'The Daily Telegraph' dated September 25, 2021. The reporter, a former soldier in Northern Ireland, recounted how he spoke to some of the youth in Tiger Bay. One young lad, who seemed to truthfully represent their views, said; *"We are the LOST OF THE LOST. They have taken away our identity."*

How sad are such words!

May the Lord bless the folk of the 'Jesus Saves' church as they shine their light in a dark place.

Chapter 14

Out on the road

We have been blessed by conducting coach tours throughout our ministry, frequently when funds were low, the opportunity to lead a coach tour brought very welcome relief. Often we were delighted to visit holiday resorts, which were entirely new to us. Our first such holiday trip was in 1987. When we were serving in Randalstown, we were invited to conduct a coach tour to Torquay in the English Riviera by C.F. Travel, Ballymena.

We were extremely grateful to the senior travel partner, E.V Hutchinson for this unique opportunity. The 10-day holiday ministering to a wonderful group of people from different denominations throughout Ulster, was very uplifting for Doreen, myself and our young son, Philip.

Upon arriving in South Belfast Elim, we had the joy of setting up meetings for the older folk. This included bringing this older group out on various day excursions to places of interest, using the church's own bus. This bus proved very useful also for Sunday school and youth work.

In later years in Lisburn Elim, we set up the '*Happiness and Harmony Club*' for the over 50's, who greatly enjoyed the day trips here and there.

When at Lisburn, we were introduced to Mr Richard McFadden from Moneyreagh, who is the proprietor of *Christian Fellowship Holidays* to Israel and elsewhere. This gentleman and his wife showed great kindness to us and gave us wonderful opportunities to lead coach tours to various parts of the world.

We remained greatly indebted to our dear brother; he certainly blessed many full-time workers with various opportunities. We recall wonderful working-holidays such as Lake Garda, 2004; Isle of Wight, 2005; The European capitals and Switzerland, 2006.

Among the European holidays, the trip to Lake Garda is remembered with both gratitude and joy. This was a particularly wonderful trip for two of our Lisburn church friends called Ida and Paul. That year, they had planned to go to Lake Garda and celebrate their 25th wedding anniversary. However, a few weeks before their holiday, Paul broke his leg and the insurance company would not cover him for his flight.

Thankfully, Mr McFadden came to the rescue by saying that they could travel on the same coach as ourselves to Lake Garda. This was a great comfort after the previous disappointment and we all felt this was something the Lord had arranged. For a long time afterwards, Ida said that this was the best holiday they ever had. While we were there, Doreen and I also celebrated our 40th wedding anniversary and the folk kindly gave us surprise gifts.

The Christian Fellowship tours to Israel were also unforgettable. We first went with Mr Richard McFadden, on an educational tour to Israel. I recall the Israeli guide rather proudly saying that they had the original Israeli scriptures, which could be translated in various ways.

Their scholars, he alleged, were the experts and he doubted whether our scriptures were accurate translations. When it came my turn to speak on the boat trip on Lake Galilee, I was determined to answer his statement.

Meanwhile, I asked him about the Jewish expectation of the coming Messiah. He said they expected him to come and deliver them '*at the great battle.*' On the boat trip, I pointed out that the best Jewish scholars 2000 years ago had informed King Herod, from their own scriptures, that the Messiah would be born in Bethlehem, according to Micah, the prophet. And then posed this question; "*If Jesus is not the Messiah, whatever happened that his arrival has been omitted and that Jews now think only of His coming at Armageddon?*"

The guy could not answer.

We were pleased to lead further Holy Land tours in 2005 and 2008. During our trips there in 2003 and 2005, we were particularly blessed by the tenor solos of Mr Sydney Hampton. Tragically Sydney died in the spring of 2008 and we attended his Thanksgiving service in Lurgan Baptist Church on March 18, 2008. These trips to Israel were extremely enjoyable and informative. We brought back many artefacts, which are still very useful in explaining the scriptures today. We had great joy in baptising people in the River Jordan, accompanied by music from Mr Jim Mitchell. Indeed the Mitchell family and friends from Banbridge provided beautiful harmonious music and songs at various Israeli venues.

'And even to your old age I am he...'

Another feature throughout the years has been our ministry in nursing homes. This work commenced in the Randalstown area in nursing homes owned by Dr. Cecil Stewart. I spoke regularly in one nursing home during the 1980's, and had the privilege of prayerfully opening a new nursing home when Dr. Stewart of CCN and his wife were present.

Upon relocating to South Belfast Elim, we assisted in a Sandy Row nursing home, from time to time. Mrs Minnie Jackson and Mr Davey Hughes had already established a ministry to the older folks in that home. When we were stationed in Lisburn, we were frequently invited to take the Sunday afternoon meetings in a local nursing home.

Opportunities then arrived to minister in Elim's nursing home in the outskirts of Hillsborough. This home was called Lisadian nursing home. I also prayed for those who were confined to their beds and were unable to attend the meetings.

Doreen, accompanied by a few ladies from Lisburn Elim, ministered faithfully over a period of years in Rose Lodge nursing home.

Occasionally musicians and singers from the church, including men would assist her. Not being able to sing did not deter her. The biggest thing for Doreen was fellowship with the people and presenting God's Word. We were all very amused when one Christmas, they presented Doreen with a cheque which was made out to the alleged Lisburn Elim choir! Her years of ministry were greatly appreciated, but she could not sing, and there was no choir!

Ironically following Doreen's death, her best friend, Hilda, suffered a severe and crippling stroke and ended up in Rose Lodge. Hilda expressed great appreciation upon recently receiving a copy of my poetry book; 'A Life Lived With Love.' This moving book is a tribute to the consecrated life Doreen lived in the service of her Lord and is designed to help people recover from bereavement.

In the midst of all the activities in various churches, the circle of family life moves on. In the last few years of his life, Mr David Swindell, Doreen's father, sadly developed cancer. We prayed much for David, especially about his salvation. Following one serious operation, my father went with Doreen and myself to visit him in hospital. My father surprised me with his very soft and kindly approach to David. Together, they conversed about heaven and home, and the need to get ready to meet the great Creator. To our great surprise and joy, David responded there and then, asking the Lord to have mercy upon him. Not long afterwards and for several weeks, he drifted in and out of consciousness.

All of his life, David had relied upon public transport and was in the habit of sticking out his hand when the right bus came along to stop and pick him up. But now that he knew that death was imminent, in a simple act of faith while semi-conscious, he would stretch out his arm as though to stop the transport.

When he awoke, he would say; *"Am I not away yet?"*

Within two years of taking ill, he died at the age of 79, on August 8, 1979, with the peace of God filling his soul. How we praise God for His great mercy and grace!

Norman with his book

Chapter 15

Until we meet again

While I was still working in BP, I visited my mother regularly who sadly in her later years, suffered with osteoarthritis.

I recall one Sunday morning as I was worshipping in Bethesda, I knew the Lord's hands were upon me and I started to prophesy; *"Do you hear the sound of the trumpets another heroine welcomed home...."*

I realised that my mother would soon be taken home to heaven and receive a glorious welcome. My brother David, realised what was being said and ran out of the church in considerable distress. It should be explained that David had no children and was therefore more emotionally attached to his mother.

About a fortnight later, my father rang me and said; "Can you come, I think your mother is dying." In fact, she was already dead.

We all gathered around her frail body. In all honesty, I had no heart to pray for her as she was 78 years of age and had spent the last 11 years crippled with excruciating pain. However, I felt I had no choice but to please the old man and so I reluctantly prayed. It was as if I could hear my mother saying within; *"How could you ask me to come back?"* My beloved mother died on September 7, 1981.

Some of my work colleagues attended her funeral service in Bethesda Elim church. I found the service very trying and emotional, but was greatly helped by the singing of that wonderful hymn; *"Face to face, shall I behold Him, far beyond the starry sky."*

One thing that my mother's passing underlined for me was that if the Lord takes us home through death, we shall receive what the bible calls, 'an abundant entrance into glory.'

We often hear about people expressing the desire to go up with the church in the rapture, but there is a lot to be said about a personal welcome.

In her younger days, my mother served in the Salvation Army's Corps as a young people's Sergeant Major, for she just loved working with children. 'The Sunbeams,' was the name of a group of children that she became involved with.

When I was stationed many years later, in the Elim church in South Belfast, it certainly wasn't very sunny, at the beginning!

Through the ACE Scheme, we befriended a lady, Mrs Sloan who was very hard on Christians. The church started to visit with her to offer help. I recall saying to her one day; *"I could do with someone like you in my church; you could set a standard!"*

I was amazed when she told me; *"That's because I was brought up in the Sunbeams, Hilda Burrows was in charge of me!"* Hilda Burrows was the name of my mother.

One day Mrs Sloan was trying to paint a room in her flat when she fell and broke her arm. I received a telephone call to go and see her. I then had the joy of leading one of my mother's original 'Sunbeams,' to the Lord.

It's true to say that when we reach our middle years, there comes a time when the previous generation seems to pass on.

Doreen's mother, Mrs Jane Swindell continued to live all alone in her little flat. One day when she became acutely depressed as she was still mourning for her late husband, she began to think seriously about taking her own life. Mercifully, a faithful city missionary felt led to visit her on that particular day and successfully persuaded her to continue living.

One day, while ironing in her home on the Shankill Road, this Presbyterian lady had a vision of the nail-pierced outstretched hands of the Saviour, who said; *"For you, for you."*

She replied: *"For me, for me, Lord?"*

And then a few days later, she attended a gospel meeting and surrendered her life to the Lord.

Sadly, Doreen's mother died from stomach cancer in the Marie Curie hospital at age 82 on July 17, 1986. On the evening of her death, it was not possible to communicate with her, so I went to the other side of the ward and spoke to a certain Mrs Childs about her need of the Saviour. This critically-ill lady responded immediately and after praying the sinner's prayer of repentance, said: *"Oh, that feels so much better! I must tell my husband when he comes to visit me."*

A few days later, she died. So the Lord was merciful again.

In respect of my father, Pastor Richard Christie senior, he continued to minister as the pastor of Bethesda Elim church.

I recall he was always a good guy for a crisis. When things were falling apart, he steadfastly believed that prayer was the answer and God would always give him the victory. However, his life was not the same and he mourned every day since the passing of my mother. Despite his great faith in Divine healing, he sadly watched our mother suffer from osteoarthritis, enduring 11 years of excruciating, crippling pain before she passed away. Despite missing my mother desperately, he lived to the ripe old age of 96. He always loved to adjust the modern saying by telling us; *"Behind every successful man is an astonished woman!"*

In his latter years, he was greatly helped by the close attendance of my brother Richard. As his health permitted, he attended New Mossley Elim church. However, gradually, his health deteriorated. On March 7, 2001, he departed this life.

He had a special Thanksgiving service held in the Ulster Temple in Belfast.

It would seem us Christie's have longevity in us as my uncle Willie also lived to a good age, passing on August 10, 2008 at 95 years of age.

Thinking about the other side of the family, we recall Hilary marrying into the Johnston family. Her husband Roy's father, Mr Sydney Johnston, who had been very active as a builder all his life, suddenly passed away on December 3, 1993. Following his death, his wife, Mrs Pearl Johnston, died from cancer on August 16, 1997. Concerning their deaths, there was a great comfort in knowing that they were right with the Lord. I had the privilege of leading them on Roy's birthday back to the Saviour. Despite her acute suffering, Pearl was comforted by her new grandchild Cherith, who was full of life and joy. In addition, the practical love and support which Roy gave to his terminally ill mother was truly amazing.

Joyous occasions...
I am pleased to write about the pleasant subject of the marriages of my four children, my three daughters Sharon, Hilary and Pamela and my son Philip.

Hilary and Roy were the first to be married on July 15, 1991, in South Belfast Elim, followed by our eldest daughter Sharon who married David on September 21, 1995, in Lisburn Elim church.

Pamela and Kyle married on August 3, 1996, in South Belfast Elim.

Both were very committed to the Lord's work, before and after their marriage. Lastly, Philip married Nadine on July 9, 2003.

I had the privilege of marrying all my children which was a great joy for myself and Doreen.

At one stage the families began a singing group called *'Youth Connection,'* whose beautiful harmonious singing was greatly appreciated in a number of churches.

Chapter 16

Raising the next generation

One of the greatest joys of later life was the arrival of our grandchildren.

Our first grandchild Cherith was born on July 11, 1995. What an exciting time to come as it was bonfire night here in Ulster! Our home was packed with young people from the church, who were enjoying the prospect of a party that evening. However for the new granny Doreen, nothing else mattered, but the fact that she had to go immediately to see baby Cherith and the new mother, Hilary. We managed to get through the festivities and greet mother and baby in the Royal Victoria Hospital.

We were thankful to learn that both mother and child were well and the dad, Roy, had survived the trauma of the birth very cheerfully.

Later, she was named Cherith Jayne, meaning; *'beloved gift of God.'*

As new grandparents we were absolutely thrilled and thankful to the Lord for her safe arrival. At the age of 15, Cherith wrote; *"I have been a granddad's girl since day one. Like granddad, I love Christmas and music.*

I have my granddad's eyes but my daddy's smile. I have some wonderful memories of granddad and I."

Cherith's first word was *'Gand,'* which was short for grandad. She currently continues to bless many people with her music and song, while studying in university for her Master's in music therapy. We all rejoiced in 2021, when Cherith obtained her M.A. degree from Cardiff University.

The next lovely girl to arrive was Rebekah Jayne Elizabeth. Born to my eldest daughter Sharon and her husband, David. Her full name means; *'pacified, gift of God, oath of God.'* She is frequently involved in good causes, at home and abroad. Rebekah is kind and caring, much loved by David's parents, Bob and Beth. In recent times, I have been writing poems for my grandchildren, upon the occasion of their 21st birthdays.

I penned this poem for Rebekah…

The apple of her father's eye,
Of this, some might wonder why,
Yet the truth is plain for all to see,
She is a source of fun and glee.

Growing up bright and sharp,
She even sings like a lark.
Affectionate and loving too,
Her Christian faith shining through.

So, like her mum, though not petite,
Tall and slim, and rather neat,
'Bekah' as she was affectionately known,
Around the world, soon was flown.

To graduate in law is her desire,
Not mediocre, but a high flyer,
When she stands up to defend your case,
From up her sleeve, expect an ace.

Following the writing of this poem, Rebekah obtained a 1st Class honours in her law degree from Trinity College, Dublin.

Benjamin was the first boy to arrive on the scene. He was a blue-eyed, blond-haired baby of the new millennium, being born January 5, 2000 to Hilary and Roy. Needless to say, he became a great favourite of the old ladies at the church. They sat in the row behind him waiting for the inevitable smile when he turned to face them. Like the two girls before him, Benjamin became a believer when he was quite young and showed considerable enthusiasm for Christianity and sport. His full name is Benjamin Philip Roy, which means; *'Son of my right hand, warrior, king.'* Now attending university Bible College, he is following God's call into ministry. My poem for him was;

> *There was a bright laddie called Ben,*
> *Who could do things beyond our ken,*
> *In making dinners, he does very well,*
> *And in other tasks, he can really excel.*
>
> *One day poor Granda phoned in a panic*
> *The fish tank was leaking and he couldn't stop it.*
> *Bold Ben arose with spanner in hand,*
> *Stopping the leak, was his clear plan.*
>
> *The carpet was wet and the towels soaked,*
> *But our hero Ben refused to choke,*
> *Saving rare fish was top priority,*
> *So Ben took over with cool authority.*
>
> *Straining youthful muscles with all his might,*
> *Filter nuts were soon made tight.*
> *The leak was stopped and Granda relieved,*
> *Both were glad when this was achieved.*

Now saving the fish was really good,
But there are others if he would,
For Jesus said it, so I know it's true,
Fishing for souls is what Ben must do.

Presently doing studies with the rest,
Our young Benjamin is trying his best,
Looking to the Lord is what he must do,
Proving JEHOVAH-JIREH to see him through.

Katherine Alexandra was born on March 15 2001, to Sharon and David. Katherine has a bright, bubbly personality and is an excellent singer. She is a member of the Irish Gospel Choir and blessed us all by bravely singing a solo at Doreen's funeral service. Katherine is successfully pursuing an academic career at Ulster University. Katherine's name means; *'pure,'* and Alexandra means; *'defending men.'* Bearing in mind that Katherine is studying law, her name seems almost prophetic.

Joshua Kyle was born to his parents, Pamela and Kyle on November 9, 2001. He is a brightly coloured red-head, whose pleasant disposition makes him very good company. His name means; *'Jehovah saves!'* At an early age, Joshua chose to serve the Lord. Having gained work experience at a primary school, this gentle giant decided that teaching young children was the calling and career for him. Now at university, he has successfully adapted to the challenges. His affectionate appreciation of his family, commitment and devotion to church life are a great blessing to us all.

Abigail, who is Joshua's baby sister, was born on the morning of September 21, 2004. If that wasn't enough excitement, her cousin, Annie was born in the afternoon of the same day to Roy and Hilary, at the same hospital. Granny Doreen found it all a bit overwhelming for one day. However visitation was a lot easier though mothers and children were on separate floors. Subsequently, it was gratifying to observe that Abigail was like her other granny Kathleen, whereas Annie favoured granny Doreen. Abigail was named, Abigail Ruth, meaning; *'Father rejoices, compassionate.'* Annie was given, Annie Megan Christine, meaning; *'Grace, Pearl, Christian one.'* They both lived on the same street, a few doors from each other. They both have attended the same schools and in many ways, are more like sisters than cousins. Both girls inspire their respective churches with music and song. However as GCSE exams approached, they chose different subjects for A-levels.

It will be interesting to see what different careers they choose to follow.

Ella and her brother, Matthew, were born to my son Philip and Nadine. Ella arrived on May 29, 2007, and Matthew on November 19, 2010, which is also my birthday! Nadine had difficulty in not having her second baby, so one day I prayed and told her God's favour was upon her and nine months later, baby Matthew was born! Ella's full name is Ella Grace, meaning; *'light, goodwill.'* Matthew's full name is Matthew Alan Norman, meaning; *'gift from God, handsome, man from the North.'* Ella is bravely overcoming certain disadvantages and maturing into a caring, affectionate girl. Matthew is a typical boy, mischievous, sport-loving and fearless.

How I thank God for His mercy in granting me nine wonderful grandchildren who delight in the things of God.

Chapter 17

The Philosophy of Ministry

Having been called in my teens to preach the gospel, it was of primary importance that I should do my best for the glory of God. I remember when first called, saying to the Lord; *'How is it that you need me? There are so many preachers in Northern Ireland.'*

The awesome reply was; *"But I will put my words in your mouth."*

Indeed, for that reason I initially refrained from using the many available commentaries and prayed and studied very much, to receive a word from the Lord that would meet the needs of the people.

However, as the years went on, I increasingly got involved in background studies and the use of aids, to give a better understanding.

My first major study was the verse by verse interpretation of the book of Ezekiel. This prophetic book of the glory of God, satisfied my deep hunger for Himself. The people seemed to be blessed by the unveiling of such amazing and complicated scriptures. I believe it is necessary to have a balanced ministry which represents both the Old and the New Testaments. As the wise saying goes; *'The new is in the old concealed and the old is in the new revealed.'*

Indeed, through taking the types and shadows of the Old Testament, we can present a greatly enhanced portrait of the Lord Jesus, shining through the New Testament. Much of the misunderstanding arising from the book of Revelation, can be clarified by comparing scripture from the Old Testament. As scripture is compared with scripture, then difficult verses can be understood by the process of eliminating or adding explanations from what is already given. Certainly, we dare not base major aspects of doctrine upon one verse, but rather through many related verses, we discover what is the truth, because it all fits together like a jigsaw and in the end, this gives us an exciting picture.

Nevertheless, as the bible states in 1 Corinthians 13:12; *'For now we see through a glass, darkly; but then face to face: now I know in part; but then shall I know even as also I am known.'* Clearly, there are some things we will never understand on this side of eternity. For example, as the apostle wrote; *"Great is the mystery of godliness."* How is it that the Lord Jesus was 100% man and yet 100% God? Does the virgin birth alone teach us? Furthermore, I believe that in the study of all the scriptures, we need to be guided by the Holy Spirit.

Jesus said, *"He would lead us into all truth."* The Psalmist said in Psalm 119:99; *"I have more understanding than all my teachers, for Thy testimonies are my delight."* How true is that statement!

God does not always *'call the qualified, but he qualifies the called.'*

Nevertheless, we should understand that the Lord has appointed godly teachers and we ought to respect their doctrine, searching the scriptures like the Berean Jews to see if these things are so. (Acts 17:11)

It is worthy of note that the Holy Spirit also knows those times in our lives when we need to learn as much as we can about a certain scriptural truth. The Holy Spirit knows the future and as we humbly wait upon Him, then He will give us the instruction we need, even before satan challenges us.

Furthermore, in order that we may become spiritually-balanced believers, we must at any given time, be led by the Lord to study much-needed scripture. As the late English Anglican vicar, David Watson said; *"All Word and no Spirit, we dry up; all Spirit, no Word, we blow up; Both Word and Spirit we grow up!"*

Books and themes of the Bible that I have particularly enjoyed include; *the life of Abraham, the Tabernacle, Psalms, The Song of Solomon, Life of Christ, Divine Love, Acts of the Apostles, Romans, Ephesians, Revelation, God in the workplace, the errors of 'faith and prosperity teaching,' Growing up in God,* and much more besides.

Spirit-led events...

It has been my privilege to attend many Christian conferences over the years. There have been the local annual one-day, Elim Irish conferences, involving good fellowship, some scriptural teaching, sharing of vision, resolving business and administration matters and then enjoying lunch together. In England, I attended the national Elim Conference, which lasted for several days. I was often reassured about my local church vision and teaching by Spirit-led International preachers.

Church business was discussed among the executive council and local pastors behind closed doors, usually in the afternoons. There were also many small seminaries, where experts gave a general audience the latest information concerning their subject of interest. There were also many stalls and a few shops where one could acquire specialised information on the latest equipment available.

I was further blessed over the latter years of pastoral life in attending Barnabas Church conferences. The warm fellowship with believers from various backgrounds, times of worship and excellent teaching were of an enormous benefit. At local church level we enjoyed the fellowship also of the folk of Lisburn City Church. During the time when I was chaplain to the mayor of Lisburn and the city council, their prayerful support was invaluable.

Attending their special conferences, involving prophetic speakers brought over from the USA was a tremendous blessing, especially at times when one was dealing with a crisis.

In recent times, I have been blessed to attend prophetic seminars, organised by an interdenominational group of pastors. The ministry of Pastor Sam Carson, a veteran Baptist pastor was particularly illuminating and there were also great times of blessing over the years, while attending the mid-week Elim pastoral fellowship meetings in Portrush. The initial organiser, Pastor McComb, called these meetings, *'advance,'* rather than *'retreat'* for obvious reasons. In the latter years under Pastor Michael's leadership, these meetings were held in Ballymascanlon hotel in Dundalk, making them more accessible to the leaders in the South.

I also enjoy attending the *'Wondrous Bible week,'* held yearly in the Ulster University in Jordanstown. It brings hundreds of people together from many denominations. The crowds have been thrilled over the years by outstanding ministry from Greg Haslem, Edwin Michael, Malcolm Duncan, Dr John Andrews and Dr Steve Brady etc. It is always a joy to meet old friends and listen to excellent preaching.

Chapter 18

Leaders to encourage by example

(Pastor John Lancaster, permission granted)

I recall listening to Pastor John Lancaster at the Elim conference in 1990. He was speaking on Psalm 110 and expanding on it in a most remarkable way. In connection with what he was teaching, I received what seemed to be an almost personal charge from Ezekiel 40:4, which ends with these words; *"Declare all that thou seest to the house of Israel,"*

In obedience, I not only took notes, but declared the message to various congregations, using acetate sheets via an overhead projector.

I give an account of part one of his sermon series…
"Leadership and the need for leaders to encourage by example!"
The day of God's power; *'Thy people shall be willing in the day of thy power"* Psalm 110:3.

- How this speaks of the great commission and coming revival!
"This is a wonderful prophetic Psalm concerning the Lord Jesus. However, our main purpose in this particular study in verse three, is to apply the word to our day and situation. The picture here is of the warrior king going forth to battle, followed by a host of followers, dedicated to him."

Like many weary pastors coming to a much-needed conference, how reassuring it was to be reminded of the captain of the Lord's host in front.

1. Every day is the day of God's power.

Because every day, all things are upheld by the word of his power. Hebrews 1:3
- Glad to be reminded that His word is an all powerful, creative Word.

Creation itself is under his control. Job 26:7
- If He holds the world upon nothing, He can surely hold us up in the storms of life.

Every embryo received life from Him. Psalm 139:14-16
- How thrilling it is to know that such is His infinite loving care, that even in the embryo stage, he carefully fashions us.

2. The Days of the Lord.

There are also special days in Psalm 77:10-12. David recalls the days of God's power. The day of Noah's embarkation, the day of delivering his people from Egypt and the day the fire fell on Mount Carmel, spring to mind.
- How easy it is easy to remember the past with envious eyes but such days should inspire us to believe for our day and generation.

a) There are Old Testament days of power but there are also New Testament days of power. For example, when Christ was born of a virgin, the day of His resurrection, the day of Pentecost.
- On these three great occasions, the common factor is the Holy Spirit at work. That same powerful life-giving Spirit is with us today.

b) Days of great revival in church history. For example, October 31st, 1517, when Luther posted his 95 theses on the door of the castle's church in Wittenberg.
- When things seem hopelessly dark and corrupt, God raises up his leaders.

c) On the day when Latimer and Ridley died on the burning stake, Latimer encouraged Ridley saying; "We have lit this day a candle,

which by God's grace, shall never be put out."
- It has been rightly said that the blood of martyrs is the seed of the church.

d) The Irish revival of 1859

e) The Welsh Revival of 1904.
- It is good to remind ourselves of what God has done in the past, He is able to do today.

f) The continuing worldwide Pentecostal revival, which began in the 1900s at the Charles Parham Bethel Bible College in Topeka, Kansas.
- How I thank God for the Pentecostal baptism of the Holy Spirit, without which I would never have entered into His high and holy calling.

3. We are living today in the day of God's power.

It is estimated that over 55 thousand souls will be saved today and every day. It is reckoned that over 2 billion Christians are alive in the world today. Are we aware of what God is doing in the world today?

a) In the time of Christ, Jerusalem did not know the day of the visitation and lost it. It's possible through unbelief, worldliness, etc. to miss the blessing, even on the day of revival. Are you prepared to be committed to His Word?
- Recently I was blessed in Zambia to observe that they hoped to establish 100 churches in two years, and they looked like they were going to achieve it. "Thy people shall be willing in the day of thy power." Quoting Isaiah 6, we read; "Who will I send and who will go for us?" A harvest of souls awaits the faithful labourers.
- May the Lord enable us to not only hear His call, but respond positively, like Isaiah.

Conclusion...

Having remembered the day of God's power in part one, Pastor Lancaster in part two, considered leadership abilities. Then, in parts three through to five, the willing people. Finally from verse seven, Pastor Lancaster declared the sufferings, the resurrection and exaltation of Christ. What a glorious unforgettable series!

Reflecting further on the teaching of these various conferences, I am blessed to consider, for example, the teaching of R.T Kendall and in particular about 'the anointing.' From 1 Samuel 16:1 He taught about *'Yesterday's men, today's men and tomorrow's men.'* It was very challenging indeed.

As much as these vary, these times of fellowship, prayer and teaching are needed by everyone.

Chapter 19

The importance of a prophetic ministry

We are distinctly told in 1 Thessalonians 5:20; *"Despise not prophesying."* When I pointed this out to a secessionist friend, he replied; *"But we have the Word of God."*

Indeed, we do and the Word is of paramount importance, is inerrant and always, our final point of reference for truth. However, that same precious Word of God tells us in 1 Corinthians 14:1; *"Follow after charity, and desire spiritual gifts, but rather that ye may prophesy."*

Do we know better than the Spirit of God, who has given us the Scriptures? And through these same Scriptures encourages us to prophecy? I must give glory to God and testify that on numerous occasions while under great pressure, I have been greatly comforted and exhorted through receiving a Holy Spirit inspired message. This can come in the form of excellent preaching, but also through the gift of prophecy, when there is frequently given a personal uplifting message. Sadly, many in the church have been denied this very direct means of comfort, due to unbelief.

I have found it particularly helpful while attending conferences and not being personally known to the speaker, to find comfort and clarification through a personal prophetic utterance. I'm also persuaded that such revelation, at times and personal exhortation of the Spirit are not confined only to Pentecostal assemblies.

Is the call of God as given personally to Barnabas, and Saul in Acts 13:2, no longer applicable? Before entering full-time ministry, I recall preaching on one occasion and afterwards praying for certain young people. Upon reaching out to one young man completely unknown to me, I said to him; *"Are you aware that God has called you into His work?"* He replied; *"Yes I am, I am studying in the Baptist Bible College."* How greatly comforted he felt and indeed through God's Word in Acts 14:22, we might all be comforted, according to God's will.

I recall in particular, the very real challenges of having to extend and refurbish Lisburn Elim church in the very early years of the new millennium. Initially I was standing upon God's Word, and the command given to me from Ezekiel 4:1 in 1984; *"you also Son of Man, pick up a brick"* GNB. This scripture I received at the time of the building of a new church by my brother Richard, and when asking the Lord to also help me build a church for His glory.

In the middle of planning in 2002 for the refurbished church and the increase in size by two and a half times, I incurred considerable problems and not a little opposition within the church itself. While attending conferences, I was greatly reassured by prophetic ministry.

On one particular occasion the speaker invited all the pastors present to come forward. The speaker called 'Rocky' from South Africa, then said; *"Who's having trouble with the local planning authorities?"* I knew that was me. I acknowledged my need to him, because I was in trouble with the planning office. He then prophesied over me that God would resolve the problems. I believed, and rejoiced to this day, for that word being wonderfully fulfilled.

Chapter 20
The impossible dream

Whatever the difficulties might be, it was evident that Lisburn Elim church needed to be extended and refurbished. Such were the drawbacks in the original building's construction, which was carried out completely by volunteers from the previous occupants, we realised that by modern standards there were aspects of the building that were actually illegal.

Following a break-in, we had a consultation with our insurance people and fears arose that the insurance cover might be withdrawn if major action was not taken. The church led by myself and Roy Johnston began prayerfully considering what the next steps should be.

Meanwhile, we were grateful for the skill of Mr Paul Smith, who carried out vital provision of metalwork construction to make the building safer and the kitchen more suitable for church dinners, etc.

Indeed the skills of various church members, under the leadership of Mr Tom Tate, continued to enhance the church premises and promote essential changes. Finally, in November 2002, both pastors produced an illustrated newsletter which was distributed to the members of the church to illustrate some of the problems facing us.

This highlighted our dependence on the good Lord, and the spiritual promises to see us through what was really an impossible task by human standards. The work was urgent, the finances were missing and the demands of our children and youth work were unrelenting.

Understandably, some church members regarded the whole project as a mere pipe-dream and the product of an ageing pastor's mind. Much time was spent at church AGM's, etc. to counteract the natural fears, and assure the folk, about the reasonable progress that had been made.

The construction of Lisburn Elim complex was beginning to become a reality. Having been advised about the excellent services of a Christian architect, Mr William Shannon, the church Oversight Committee met with him in May 2003, when planning commenced.

During the planning stages, Pastor McComb enquired by telephone about the validity of the whole project, He asked; *"Tell me Norman is all this viable?"* My reply was; *"Well, Eric, you would not attempt it, unless you had faith."*

It was interesting to note that Pastor McComb considered our project the most *'financially tight'* of all of his experiences of church renovations.

Key verses that guided us through the development of the building programme were Isaiah 54:2-3; *"Enlarge the place of thy tent, and let them stretch forth the curtains of thine habitations: spare not, lengthen thy cords, and strengthen thy stakes; For thou shalt break forth on the right hand and on the left; and thy seed shall inherit the Gentiles, and make the desolate cities to be inhabited."* The words of verse three; *"right hand and on the left,"* proved to be critical.

At the time of preparation, we had a narrow driveway on the right of the building, however, through negotiations with the owners of the apartment complex next door, we were granted leave to widen the driveway in phase one. Just as well, because as we began to replace the retaining wall, we discovered that it was about to collapse into the next door's premises. Furthermore, in the latter stages of building in phase two, the only route open to the 100 foot cranes was to come down that widened driveway. Truly we rejoiced in God's guidance in this, and in many other matters, in which we were saved from a disaster.

Sadly, some people who misunderstood the details of the project stopped tithing. When I asked the treasurer how much money was missing, he said; *"£8,000."* The cost of the project at that stage was also £8,000. The bill was due to be paid by Christmas but we therefore couldn't pay it.

Fortunately the builder went on holiday abroad for several weeks, but when he returned we were able to pay.

Further promises which inspired us to believe in God, were Nehemiah 2:18; *"Then I told them of the hand of my God which was good upon me; as also the king's words that he had spoken unto me. And they said, Let us rise up and build. So they strengthened their hands for this good work."* Habakkuk 2:2-3; *"And the Lord answered me, and said, Write the vision, and make it plain upon tables, that he may run that readeth it. For the vision is yet for an appointed time, but at the end it shall speak, and not lie: though it tarry, wait for it; because it will surely come, it will not tarry."* Isaiah 60:13; *"and I will make the place of my feet glorious."*

In respect of the major stages of the building, we were grateful to God for sending a young businessman and his family from the south of Ireland to our church, and enabling this generous-hearted man to pay the necessary fees at critical times, when we just didn't have the money.

At that time we were also grateful for Mr Stephen Mc Master, who produced a model of the extended church. At this time we had to stop building in order to organise the £200,000 deposit. A trying period of three years passed by. Our plans, which were passed in 2005, expired in 2008, leaving us with new building regulations and a possible 10% increase in the overall price.

It was also the time of the International recession. Thanks to the diplomatic negotiations of our architect, it was accepted that through the construction of our phase one that the building was deemed as having commenced. The new building charges therefore did not apply.

This was certainly an answer to prayer.

As described at the conference, promising help earlier, we proceeded to approach our new bank, First Trust Lisburn, who treated us with every possible courtesy. The names of their co-operating bank managers, Uel and Judith remain gratefully fixed in my mind. Our initial application for a loan was accepted and reckoned to be about the maximum we could afford. However, upon going to tender for business purposes, the resulting business costs were much higher than expected. As a result, the Treasurer suggested new plans for a smaller building. But when such new ideas were submitted to the builder, the reduction in price was minimal. The majority of the church session thought that we should therefore keep to the original plans.

We remembered the words of D L Moody, "*If God is with you, then make your plans big!*" Besides, I strongly felt that the Lord was in the original plans, and we ought not to change, *"the pattern as shown."* Nevertheless, the facts were now clear that the total cost of the building would finally amount to £1.2 million.

I vividly recall approaching the bank again, with one of our businessmen, at the time of the recession in 2008. In requesting an ever greater bank loan, we were desperately hoping and praying for a miracle. To my utter amazement and gratitude, my further loan request from the bank was granted. The next vital step was the necessary agreement of Elim headquarters in England to sanction our proposals, because they were the guarantors.

At this stage, our local superintendent, Pastor Eric McComb, believed God and fully supported our risky venture and negotiated successfully for the project to go ahead.

Our builders, T&A Kernoghan were officially to begin work in January 2009. The Lord had answered prayer, and we were gratefully relieved in a very stressful situation. The project involved major changes, including the positioning of a lift, which was also required for the disabled to access every floor. The overall area of the original church was to be increased by approximately two and a half times.

At the wise advice of the local Elim executive, we were instructed to vacate the existing old building while renovations were taking place. We were extremely grateful to Lisburn CWU, who allowed us to use their premises rent free. This meant that virtually all our church ministry and activities continued unhindered.

Notably, a future Elim pastor, Phil Seifert and his wife, Eneide, joined us while we were based in the CWU Hall. Upon returning to the newly-finished building, I was requested to take under my wing, Mr Stuart Argue, who was then in training to become a pastor. He turned out to be an excellent probationer, whose diligent compassion and concern for the people of all ages was really an inspiration. His fine preaching and fellowship were a great source of comfort to me during difficult times.

In 2006, we had been greatly blessed for several months, with the Ministry of Mr and Mrs Roy Walker, and 'Spud Murphy' from *Crown Jesus Ministries*. Roy spoke words of wisdom into the heart of the church at the controversial time when we were planning to build. Brother Murphy was the 'ideas man' who enabled us to more effectively reach the people in the local community. We praise God for *Crown Jesus Ministries*, which continue to do such amazing work for the Lord in our country.

In 2006 we also said a sad farewell to pastor Roy Johnston, Hilary and family upon their appointment to lead Beersbridge Road Elim church.

They had very diligently and loyally served at Lisburn Elim from 1994 until 2006. They had specialised in ministry to young marrieds, youth and young children. During that time, Roy had also served for six years on the Elim youth committee, and a further four years as Elim youth director.

On completing 10 years in Lisburn, he was then appointed as a member of the Irish Elim executive while continuing his excellent ministry among us. During this time, he served as chaplain to the Distillery football team, doing a great work among them. We also appreciated his gospel preaching, Bible studies and very conscientious ministry of pastoral care to the people.

While holding down a responsible teaching post in a local primary school, Hilary faithfully served the Lord and her family, excelling in leading worship, music ministry and drama, not to mention the church choir. Hilary's creativity was superb! On occasions, Doreen and I greatly enjoyed having their toddler Cherith, our granddaughter, to visit members of the congregation, because her delightful personality uplifted several depressed people.

Nevertheless, when God is blessing, satan is always opposing. But the Lord answers! For despite acute problems and gross disloyalty from some quarters, a beautiful, purpose-built complex finally emerged and the Lord who triumphs was also glorified. Today, this outstanding building has received much acclaim for the learning and promotion of Elim's future leaders through the Academy, which regularly meets there. Upon completion of the complex, a stainless-steel plaque was placed on the wall, bearing the words of 1 Samuel 7:12 *"Hitherto hath the Lord helped us."*

For with God, nothing is impossible...

Now while all this was happening, we enjoyed close fellowship with Pastor Brian Agnew, his wife, Mary and the folk in Kingdom Life City Church. Indeed we shared water baptismal services in our church and rejoiced together over new converts from both fellowships.

When I was appointed Chaplain by Alderman Paul Porter, Lisburn City's new mayor in 2010, the leadership of Kingdom Life provided much prayer and spiritual support. During the 12 months of holding that post, it was a great privilege for me to share both prayer and spiritual gifts with the members of Lisburn City council.

Following the opening of the new complex on Saturday, September 5, 2009, a potentially embarrassing situation arose. We had no money to pay for the first monthly instalment due to the bank which had treated us so considerably well. Urgent prayer was made and to our great relief and utter amazement, a gentleman came to the church and put in his six months tithes, which he had accumulated while searching for a place to worship.

That was all we needed so we cheerfully gave thanks to God.

The amazing conclusion to all this is simply the fulfilment of the Scripture in Luke 1:37; *"For with God nothing shall be impossible."*

One of the extras in the refurbished building was the provision of a wooden ramp to make access to the platform for the disabled. This ramp proved to be invaluable for the transportation of very heavy equipment onto the platform. We were favoured with the brilliant music skills of Mr Steven McLaughlin, who for special occasions, would bring a grand piano onto the platform using this ramp.

As the American poet, Edwin Markham said; *"Great it is to dream the dream, when you stand in youth by the starry stream; but a greater thing is to fight life through and say at the end, the dream is true!"*

The church initially had hoped to incorporate a boardroom, in the renovated building, where the session could meet. However, when the plans were drawn up, such a room could not be incorporated into the design. However, in the process of the actual refurbishment, a substantial gap was discovered over the foyer of the old building.

Suddenly we discovered an amazing, surprising opportunity to create a boardroom, where there previously had been a void. This subsequent boardroom having a new circular window proved to be a beautiful, delightful place to meet. When the room was finished it became suitable for many activities. As the scriptures say in Ephesians 3:20-21; "*Now unto him, that is able to do exceeding abundantly above all that we ask or think, according to the power that worketh in us. Unto him be glory in the church by Christ Jesus throughout all ages, world without end. AMEN.* "

An original building of dubious mission hall status, was transformed into a high-tech modern, church complex. All this the Lord brought to birth in nine months, under the leadership of a 68-year-old pastor, whose knowledge of finance, modern design and technology was minimal. Following the arrival of a new pastor, which occurred after the building was completed, Doreen and I stayed for a few months then finally left Lisburn Elim in 2011.

That signalled the end of our pastoral duties at the age of 71 and we then commenced freelance preaching etc. here and there, as the Lord opened doors for us.

My son-in-law Roy became the pastor at Lurgan Elim and we were pleased to join him there with my daughter Hilary and their three children. We became members of the church, being glad to make some new friends and renew friendship with others we had known for years.

Meanwhile, Doreen continued her years of service with the 'Royal Belfast Hospital for Sick Children ladies league.' Doreen met regularly with other committee members and was involved in regular fundraising for hospital projects. I quote from one of the league's newsletters; "*Mrs Christie had made aprons and had taken a stall at a school Christmas fayre where she sold them all and raised £100 - this was greatly appreciated.*"

Indeed Doreen got involved when required in this skill, and with a local Lisburn primary school, made garments etc. for school plays and was well-known and liked by the staff.

At this time we were warmly welcomed by the local Barnabas churches, whose pastors I had taught when they were young men. How gratifying it was to observe that these men, who once had secular jobs, had become outstanding men of God with International ministries!

In those days we had the privilege of ministering in several churches, on digital radio, nursing homes and various small halls. I was particularly blessed by the ministry of the Hicksons at the 2019 Barnabas conference, having received a personal prophecy which is still in process of coming to pass.

At the beginning of that same decade, we enjoyed the annual Elim conferences in England, not to mention the ordination to the pastorate of local young men in Elim. However, little did we know that the latter part of this decade would herald the passing of several family members to their awards in glory. These included Mrs Marty Christie in January 2016, Mrs Doreen Christie in October 2016, Mr William Preshaw in April 2017, Pastor David Christie, July 2017, Pastor Richard John Christie, September 2018, Mr Jim Prenter, November 2018 and Mrs Joyce Christie, July 2020.

I know that this sort of experience happens sooner or later in the lives of so many families, but how uplifting it is when you know that the Sovereign Lord is in control!

Thank God we will meet again on the other side.

Chapter 21

Enduring heartbreak

As I contemplate the passing of my precious help-meet Doreen, a couple of strange things occurred in advance. Upon choosing her September birthday card, I first saw a sympathy card, which was clearly in the wrong place, sitting among the birthday cards.

In addition, my wristwatch had been irreparably broken. Just in the week before we left for Torremolinos, Doreen decided to buy me a new watch which would serve as a gift for my November birthday party, not knowing that she would be absent.

Looking back now, we were so excited to be leaving our home that day to head to the Spanish shores. We had no idea of the huge life-changing experience that awaited.

We cheerfully headed off with our Christian party of believers under the leadership of a Baptist pastor and his wife for our trip to Spain. Doreen and I had visited the Spanish islands a few times before but this was our first visit to Torremolinos in Costa Del Sol.

When we arrived on the beautiful island, we enjoyed the fellowship and evening meetings with the others in the hotel Don Pablo.

I fondly recall one evening, Doreen laughed over and over again when the pastor's wife gave an address citing her husband's occasional dreamy actions, which proved to be very similar to mine! Like many husbands who don't always listen to what their wives are saying, Doreen often observed; *"One day they are going to take me away for talking to myself."*

It was only a couple of days later, on October 12, 2016, that tragedy unexpectedly struck.

Our lovely holiday in Spain was coming to an end and we were due to return home on that Wednesday afternoon with the other members of the touring party under the leadership of Pastor Freddy and Linda McClaughlan. We both began on Wednesday morning feeling well and happy. We went down for breakfast in the hotel, cheerfully meeting some friends on the way. However after enjoying her 'Ulster Fry' Spanish variety, Doreen complained of being hot and dizzy and thought the room was too warm.

We quickly left, and I held her hand tightly as she was very unsteady.

We sat in the foyer for a while hoping she would recover. It was apparent that Doreen was getting worse, which made us promptly head for our bedroom, where I hoped that sitting on the balcony would help. Sadly, however, things got worse. Acute nausea and pain took over.

Nearby, I found a young Spanish attendant, who very pleasantly assisted us, as we tried to cope with much vomiting and weakness. At one point Doreen said; *"I cannot see!"*

Upon complaining about her chest and arm pain, I called reception for a doctor. We had previously paused in the hope of getting the flight home in a few hours and receiving medical attention from the doctors in our family.

Fortunately the Spanish lady doctor arrived promptly just as Doreen went into convulsions. The doctor was immediately alarmed, attended to Doreen and telephoned for emergency help.

But it was all in vain, and within a few minutes, the doctor said to me that Doreen was dead. The time was 12:45pm. In an instant, my life was changed forevermore.

We thought at first that it was a heart attack, but upon coming home and describing the symptoms, the doctors in the family decided it was a brain haemorrhage resulting in heart failure.

It was all a very great shock; the Spanish doctor was most sympathetic and the young Spanish attendant returned later and wept, expressing her sorrow.

Mercifully I didn't go into shock, but felt a strange sorrowful peace as the dreadful loss began to sink in. I thought about all the precious times I had shared with Doreen and also about the wonderful children she had blessed me with. I do not know how long I sat recounting all the wonderful times we had shared but I was aware of some commotion at the door. All the necessary officials arrived in the form of the hotel management, the undertaker's and the Spanish police. The hotel officials gave me the opportunity to stay for another week, but my priority was to get home with the rest of the touring party, knowing that because of the insurance, Doreen's body would eventually arrive home.

They also assisted me to phone home and I informed my devastated family that I was coming home without mum.

Meanwhile, Pastor Freddy and his wife returned to the hotel and immediately came to see me when they heard that Doreen had died. They both took great care of me and even arranged for my family to receive me upon arrival at the George Best Airport, Belfast.

During the forthcoming week, my family never left me alone and dozens of sympathy cards were received from our many friends.

Included among the many visitors was an elderly gentleman whose wife had died a year earlier, while with us on holiday in a touring party. He greeted me with the words; *"I see Norman, the same thing has happened to you as happened to me."*

Doreen's body arrived home on the following Friday, giving us the opportunity to get a little more used to the shock and the funeral arrangements.

A Service of Thanksgiving was held in Lurgan Elim church where she was greatly loved and appreciated. Over 500 people from across our divided community attended on Monday, October 24, 2016. It was the largest funeral service that the church had ever held and one of my neighbours said; *"There wasn't a dry eye in the place."*

As a family we were extremely grateful to all who took part, including Pastor Edwin Michael, Pastor Mark Patterson, my granddaughter Katherine, who was the soloist and my son Philip who read my tribute.

The tribute to my beloved wife...
It is with great sadness that I address you today on behalf of my family in respect of the sudden and unexpected departure to Glory of my beloved wife, our mother, grandmother and mother-in-law, Doreen.

We also acknowledge her sister Alice, brother-in-law Billy, Elaine, Jennifer and their families.

It was as a lad of 18, at my friend Sammy's birthday party, that I observed amongst the group of girls a certain pretty young lady called Doreen Swindell, whose smile and demeanour attracted my immediate attention. Instantly I thought; "There's the girl for me."

Her happy, radiant countenance and obvious warm acceptance of myself, left me spellbound – indeed it was to leave me spellbound for life.

Later, as I walked her home hand-in-hand down the Shankill Road, I perceived that there was a mutual love from which I would never depart, except God instructed me otherwise.

Having become aware of her simple faith in the Christ of whom I also trusted, it was easy for me to prayerfully continue our joyful new-found friendship. I was soon to learn that this lowly girl from Hopeton Street was both gifted and resourceful. Even the beautiful lilac dress and accoutrements which adorned her at the birthday party, had been crafted by her own hands.

Fervently, in those teenage years, Doreen served the Lord as a Sunday school teacher and Girl Guide leader, particularly in Albert Street Presbyterian church.

At that stage being the only one in her family to confess Christ as Saviour, Doreen braved the difficulties and years later would have her prayers answered in seeing all of them come to Christ.

Together, we were destined to serve the Lord as Sunday School teachers and youth leaders, not to mention Girl Guides, Brownies and Campaigners in Bethesda Elim church, right in the heart of 'The Troubles' in North Belfast.

At the age of 21 we were engaged, and later married on August 15, 1964, in Bethesda. My generous father provided us with a Morris Mini and indeed afforded us many wonderful gifts throughout his long life.

Indeed, I thank God for my late father and mother who taught us the ways of the Lord, demonstrated kindness to all, and refused to accept sectarianism.

Their obvious delight in Doreen and our four children, Sharon, Hilary, Pamela and Philip was a joy to behold.

Meanwhile, we were greatly blessed during our early holidays in Newcastle, County Down, where, as a result of team ministry, hundreds of young lives were won for Christ. By this time, I was regularly involved in lay-preaching, embracing both Roman Catholics, Protestants and non-believers. Always Doreen was there by my side, whether in Belfast, Crumlin Road, Shankill Road, Ardoyne or the notorious Armagh murder triangle etc.

At that time we joined Pastor Roy Kerr in Teen Challenge right here in Northern Ireland.

Again, it was our supreme joy to visit cross-community institutions, frequently showing David Wilkerson's great film; 'The Cross and the Switchblade,' 'The Road to Armageddon' etc. Our reception at all institutions was both wonderful and fruitful.

I was, however, most grateful to obtain a good job in the BP Oil Refinery at age 23. The laboratory work there was both diverse and interesting. Because of their excellent provision for their staff, Doreen remained at home with the children and only returned to employment several years later. We were therefore able to continue our many tasks of outreach ministry. However when BP decided to close their Belfast Refinery, then, with many others, I found myself redundant. At the time, I was holding children's meetings in a tent in New Mossley, where my brother Richard had built a new church.

My immediate decision was to serve the Lord in full-time ministry. This was a great shock to Doreen and my family, especially since our family of six was destined to lead a congregation of six stalwarts in Randalstown.

Other possibilities in secular work were available, but as ever, we acted upon the call of God and from Father God's book, Exodus chapter 21:5; "And if the servant shall plainly say, I love my Master, my wife and my children; I will not go out free."

And so, the journey continued serving the Lord as a family both in South Belfast and Lisburn, where at age 67, I had the immense privilege of updating and extending the original premises by two and a half times.

In those days, Doreen and my beloved son-in-law Roy, joined me in commencing the I.C.I College of Ulster in which many lay people from around the country were trained for the work of the Lord. Leaving church leadership at age 70, we proceeded to continue preaching in virtually every conceivable denomination. As usual, Doreen was always with me, providing refreshments, encouraging in ministry, but always bestowing her generous and radiant love upon her four children and nine grandchildren, whose hearts are broken today by her sad and sudden passing through a massive heart attack.

A great highlight of Doreen's ministry from the earliest days to retirement was her unbelieveable dinners, whether it was reception dinners for the weddings of the not-so-well-off, or evangelistic dinners at Christmas when strangers came freely. Doreen's cooking and organisation excelled.

Doreen simply loved people and exchanged words and smiles even with our critics and enemies. I sincerely thank you and on behalf of my family, express deep gratitude for every expression of sympathy and condolence, not to mention frequent visits to our home and your beautiful cards, which often brought tears by their touching words.

During the past three years of membership in Lurgan Elim, we have found Christian love, appreciation and opportunity. We have loved Pastor Mark and his wife, Merle.

What more can I say except to give God the Glory. Through our combined ages, we have enjoyed over 150 years of God's Grace and preservation. Our four gifted children and nine grandchildren have all proved God's amazing and saving Grace for themselves.

Should Doreen be able to hear this, we simply say... "Au Revoir, we have greatly loved you... See you in the morning!"

Thank you heavenly Father for lending us beloved Doreen for so long. Thank you dear Saviour for redemption. Thank you Holy Spirit, the paracletos for comforting us.

May God help us all to follow the Lord Jesus.

Refreshments took place in the church hall and Doreen was buried in Dromore cemetery, close to where most of the family now live.

Doreen is still sadly missed and my personal journey through bereavement is described in my first book; *'A Life Lived With Love.'*

Basically, it is through expressing our need for Him in prayer, that we experience the healing power of the One, who has promised to *'bind up the broken hearted.'*

Chapter 22

Walking alone

A few weeks after Doreen's death, I was required to attend a conference for ministers. Shortly before leaving, my distracted mind realised that I had run out of essential blood pressure tablets, and it was then too late to get a prescription.

After a while, I remembered that Doreen kept a supply for me in the car in case of an emergency or forgetfulness.

Sure enough, I found them there, just enough to see me safely through the conference. I recall thinking; *"Even when she is dead she's still looking after me."*

The scripture comes to mind in Proverbs 31-10; *"Who can find a virtuous woman? for her price is far above rubies."*

Following Doreen's death, it became necessary for me to make a fresh start in life. Without the joy of having her by my side, as I recounted in my first book, I discovered that writing poetry brought me some emotional relief from the dreadful devastation of bereavement.

However difficult, important decisions needed to be made. I quickly realised that my existing four bedroom family home was not only a bit too big for me, but it was filled with happy memories, which had all started to become painful. Within a few weeks, I put it up for sale.

And although it didn't sell until a couple of years later, I needed that time to distribute much of the contents.

This also gave me the opportunity not only to de-clutter, but to gather together those family treasures that might otherwise have been lost. It became my intention to move to Dromore, where most of my family were then living. Fortunately my alert daughter, Pamela noticed there was a small apartment, which had just come onto the market. We acted immediately knowing today's homes in Dromore can sell overnight.

Fortunately we secured the sale within 24 hours, and just in the nick of time before another interested party arrived.

About this time it was also necessary to contact our solicitor and get a new will prepared and to appoint a family member, as power of attorney to handle my affairs, in the event of me becoming incapacitated.

By then it was apparent that attending the same church was problematic, because I kept being reminded of Doreen's various activities etc. A few months after settling in Dromore, I joined a small local Elim fellowship in Donaghcloney. Clearly, they were pleased to receive me, and I was very glad of the new opportunities afforded to me there.

With the arrival of COVID-19. I was given opportunities, courtesy of Pastor Phil Seifert to help with the zoom and streaming of the broadcasts.

We soon developed International contacts for a small assembly. This was very exciting. Furthermore, a delightful partnership had arisen with three other churches in the time-being, a Methodist church, a Church of Ireland and the Presbyterian Church resulting in prayer meetings, and outreach together with these sincere evangelical churches which were sources of great joy and comfort.

Furthermore, teaching trips to Zambia, and the privilege of leading a group to Israel were very uplifting events. If that was not enough, becoming involved in the newly-formed interdenominational Prophetic Seminary was further testimony of the Lord's enlarging of my vision, and comforting me on every side. To God be the glory!

I moved into my new apartment in Circular Road, Dromore during the spring of 2018. This brought me close to the Dromore residences of two of my daughters and their families. It was the beginning of a new chapter of my life, when as a widower I needed to adjust to many changes and participate in a steep learning curve.

Whilst still endeavouring to cope with the memories concerning Doreen's departure, other family deaths would take their toll. My elder brother, David had died on July 31 2017, and another brother, Richard would receive his home call on September 16, 2018. Thankfully both brothers were believers, and had served gratefully as Elim pastors. Of the original family of six, there would remain just myself, and my eldest brother Leonard, who became confined to a nursing home. However I continued, although retired, to live a very active life in the service of the Lord, as is the case, even to this day.

As I recovered from the loss of Doreen, it has been a considerable joy to collect my precious grandchildren from school every day and listen to their joyful chatter, especially when we were able to visit local cafes. It is also a matter of considerable joy to me that I have the privilege of ministering in various denominations and to different age groups.

Mr Brian Graham from the Brethren Crescent church, took a considerable compassionate interest in me after Doreen's home call and introduced me to several groups of Bible scholars. It became very uplifting to fellowship and converse with these like-minded men.

Meanwhile, my old friend, Mr John Wylie encouraged me to join him and others in holding gospel concerts to raise funds for the Northern Ireland Children's Hospice.

Everywhere we went, several hundreds of pounds were raised each evening to benefit the Hospice, which very much depended on public generosity. John, being a well-known singer and guitarist in the province, introduced me to new venues, where he did the singing and I did the convening and preaching. Lots of people appeared to be blessed by our humble efforts.

Visiting distant shores…

In the summer of 2018, my son-in-law, Pastor Roy Johnston, Elim Irish Missions Director, introduced me to Pastor Ziso Moyo of Oasis Ministries, Zambia. He told us that in Zambia, the work of God is so-increasing that they are unable to provide sufficiently-trained pastors to lead the many new churches. I was asked there and then to go and teach young leaders for the work of God. I felt both humbled and challenged and replied in the affirmative. I had dreamed for years about going overseas to teach and preach, and now suddenly it was all happening!

It was planned that Roy and I would go over that year from September 26, until October 10, 2018. Consequently, the medics in the family expressed their concerns about me being exposed to the tropical diseases of Zambia. However, against their advice, I decided to trust the Lord and go, as due to the many false cults, the need for sound bible teaching was great. It was to be one of the best decisions of my life!

I had further proved God in 2017 during an exciting visit to Israel. That trip to Israel was my fourth time there, but alas, it was the first time without my wonderful wife and helper, Doreen. This time I was greatly helped and not a little comforted by the companionship of my eldest granddaughter, Cherith.

Now that visit to Israel occurred on September 4-13, 2017, and involved 15 holidaymakers. It was planned by Mr Richard McFadden of Christian Fellowship Holidays, Moneyreagh. I was so grateful that Cherith was able to come, which considerably lessened the burden of needing and caring for all these Northern Ireland folk, who came from various backgrounds and denominations.

On this trip, we were able to visit some exciting new places, such as Bethlehem and Abraham's tent area where we had camel rides; and a very special and moving experience of the Lord's presence in the prison, where Jesus was held overnight prior to His crucifixion.

This Israel holiday began with an overnight visit to the hotel, Ramada Hadar. It was a five-star hotel in Netanya, overlooking the magnificent views of the Mediterranean Sea. The scrumptious breakfast in luxurious surroundings was a healing balm to the weary travellers. Each day was packed with exciting visits to beautiful Bible locations in perfect weather conditions. We first travelled to Caesarea Maritima and I observed the Hippodrome and Herod the Great's swimming pool. Then there was the beautiful port of Haifa and its magnificent gardens against the shining backdrop of the Mediterranean Sea. Arriving by the sea of Galilee we came to Tabgha where the miracles of the five loaves and two fishes are recorded on the mosaic Church floor.

What a joy it was to visit the splendid church of the Beatitudes shortly afterwards and walk in the sunbathed gorgeous gardens!

However the trip on lake Galilee in the 'Jesus boat' was an unforgettable experience. Sharing a few thoughts from the life of Jesus was a special privilege for me on the boat, and indeed there were daily opportunities for meditation and prayer at the many sacred sites.

Our minds were further broadened by our visit to Safed. (A rabbitical holy city) There on display were beautiful works of art, particularly in the Soul Art Gallery.

Meanwhile, as we travelled, we were excited and privileged to see pomegranate trees, fig trees, date palms and all manner of exotic and beautiful flowers. For those of a historical mindset, we encountered at Beth She'an the stunning and well-preserved remains of Roman occupation.

The climate is deceptively warm in Israel and you need to drink lots of water throughout the day. Indeed in Beth She'an, one man was collapsing through heat exhaustion but we managed to give him sufficient water and he revived.

In due course, we would visit Yardenit Baptismal Site along the River Jordan. Over the years, I have had the privilege of baptising a number of folk there and presenting them with their much-prized certificates. If one is baptising in the Spring then the Jordan is surprisingly chilled by the melting snow from the peak of Mount Hermon.

Indeed, on one occasion I was concerned because two people in their 90's wanted to be baptised in the Jordan. However I am glad to say they were unharmed.

There are also in the river, large but harmless Catfish which some folk may find alarming.

In our 2017 visit, it was rewarding to at last get to Bethlehem, which for security reasons had not been previously available to us. In Bethlehem, the paintings on the walls of the church concerning the birth of Christ and the visit of the angels to the shepherds are quite exquisite. On the floor of the grotto of the Church of the Nativity, there is the golden 'Star of Bethlehem,' which is said to mark the traditional place of Jesus' birth.

It was particularly interesting at the Gate of David in Bethlehem as spoken of in 2 Samuel 23:15; *"And David longed, and said, Oh that one would give me drink of the water of the well of Bethlehem, which is by the gate!"*

Three mighty men rode through the hosts of the Philistines and delivered the water to David.

That moving narrative is like a parable of the gospel story, as we recall how the Almighty Trinity broke through all the hindrances, causing the Saviour to be born in Bethlehem.

Isaiah 12:3 sums it up so beautifully; *"Therefore with joy shall ye draw water out of the wells of salvation."*

Moving on to the area called 'Abraham's Country' the tourists were delighted to ride on camels and partake of a meal in a large tent, similar to what Father Abraham enjoyed. Travelling on to Jerusalem we were blessed with the views of the Mount of Olives, the area called Mount Zion, the Upper Room, the Via Dolorsa (the way of the cross) Golgotha, the Garden Tomb etc.

However the visit to the palaces of the High Priest containing the dungeon where Jesus was held overnight prior to His Crucifixion, had a profound effect on us all. In the dungeon, it was my privilege to read Psalm 88 which was recorded in various languages in a folder upon a little lectern. The atmosphere was very heavy with the awesome presence of God as though the tragedy of His overnight imprisonment was happening there and then, as we witnessed the chains which held Jesus.

The otherwise jovial tourists were suddenly rendered seriously burdened and unsmiling. It became evident to us that the Psalm was clearly expressing how the Saviour felt on the night before his crucifixion.

No doubt, we had all read this Psalm before, but now its tragedy and reality was breaking in upon our souls in the most extraordinary fashion. The horror of it all came upon us as such verses like verse 3 were solemnly read; *"For my soul is full of troubles: and my life draweth nigh unto the grave."*

Truly this is a Messianic Psalm which we frequently pass over. Even our Jewish guide had been affected. When I thanked him for bringing us to the place and allowing us to read the scriptures, he emphatically replied; *"It is after all, the Word of God."*

I studied late that evening and presented Psalm 88 at the next opportunity in our evening Epilogue service. Shortly afterwards, our spirits were greatly lifted when we observed the Garden Tomb with the poignant words on the door, *"He is not here, for He is risen."*

My final reference of this tour is our visit to Megiddo. This great battlefield is the biblical scene of the final stage of the battle of Armageddon. Even now Israeli planes patrol the valley 24-7 and then disappear into their hidden underground bunkers.

Our great King of Kings and Lord of Lords will finally overcome the forces of darkness. *"And He shall reign for ever and ever!"* (Revelation 11:15)

However, on this 2017 tour we missed the wonderful singing of Mr Sydney Hampton. On our previous tours Sydney had sung in his lovely tenor voice some of the beautiful old hymns such as; *'The Stranger of Galilee.'*

Even the Jews loved his singing. Sadly in 2008, Sydney who was an Elder in Lurgan Baptist Church was suddenly called home to be with his Lord and Saviour while enjoying a church outing.

Chapter 23

Following the Great Commission

Thinking further about the autumn visit to Zambia in 2018, I am glad to share further details of what proved to be an uplifting experience for all concerned.

I was indebted to Mr Roy Johnston, my son-in-law whose knowledge of International travel was invaluable, as we made our way through various cities and airports.

We were spurred on by the Saviour's Great Commission to bring the gospel to the 'Whosoever.' In those days, a famous saying lingered in our minds; *"God's church doesn't have a mission in the world. God's mission in the world, has a church!"*

We left home in Northern Ireland on Wednesday 26 September, 2018 at 9.30am, and arrived in Zambia the next day at approximately 6pm, having travelled via Dublin, Dubai and Johannesburg.

We were extremely grateful to the Emirates airline for permitting us to bring free of charge, a consignment of goods donated for the orphans at Ndola.

As dusk fell on Ndola, there to greet us was the effervescent Pastor Ziso and his smiling companion Daniel, the bible teacher. Soon we were settled in the comfortable cottage built in the garden of Pastor

Ziso's home, where he lives happily with his darling Northern Irish wife Nicki, and their three delightful children, Zach, Zoe and Zara.

We quickly adjusted to the water purification facility and overnight mosquito nets.

Next day we were introduced to the L.I.F.T Teams (Labour in Faith & Trust) from Northern Ireland, who were completing in an incredible eight days, the erection of Cichelli Oasis Church. How exciting it was to see this new attractive church built in the African style!

The L.I.F.T team was led by in this project by Tony, a builder from Ballymena. It is the fifth structure of its type, but many more are needed to accommodate the vision for 100 churches.

At that time there were 26 Oasis fellowship churches in Zambia. What a desperate need there was to train the new leaders and get church buildings erected!

Ndola has a population of 450,000, with a life expectancy of only 45 years. The native language is Bamba, but English is widely spoken.

The first impressions I got were that Zambia could be likened to a giant awakening from sleep, having enormous potential, but in danger of assault from numerous false cults. It became apparent that China had a great interest in controlling Zambia.

The Elim Christian Centre is well named as the Oasis village supplying accommodation for 53 orphans and their education in a wonderful, loving and happy Christian atmosphere. The school has 550 fee-paying pupils and free education and accommodation for the orphans.

I had the enormous privilege of teaching some 20 young leaders over a period of six days.

We covered three months of normal church instruction in that time period. The enthusiasm, singing and worship expressed by those trainees was both amazing and inspiring.

How delightful it was one afternoon, when the class was over, to walk through the grounds of the Oasis village and observe a praise leader standing on an improvised platform leading all of the orphans with impromptu singing and actions for *"oh happy day."*

One day in the classroom, I had been teaching from 9am to 6pm while enduring a tummy upset. At the end of the day I felt sick and totally exhausted but the gracious Lord filled the room with His presence and all of us were blessed, refreshed and uplifted.

At one stage Pastor Roy travelled up north with Nicki to meet Gordon McKillip, the veteran Elim missionary. He found the work there at Nyangombe to be absolutely mind-blowing!

The bible teaching, instruction of apprentices for various trades, supervision of the hydro-electric scheme, and care of the sick and needy was amazing.

For me it was a great joy to observe the excellent work done by our missionaries, but the challenges remain for us at home to send out bible teachers and practical workers, to help with what is basically a revival situation, *"the Harvest is plenteous, but the labourers are few."*

Meanwhile, we enjoyed many exciting events in Zambia, such as the joyful opening of the new church built by the L.I.F.T team in Chichele, where the local young people sang the praises of the Lord and Pastor Roy preached.

The other main church in Ndola, Oasis church was the venue for our Sunday services. The enthusiastic worship of the congregation, which consisted of largely young people, was truly inspiring. Our trip was rounded off by an amazing fireworks display, courtesy of the local grammar school and intended to raise funds for that institution.

At all times, gracious respect and gratitude were shown to Pastor Ziso, known to their orphans as 'Dad' or the 'Bishop' and his wife Nicki.

Each day I had the privilege of teaching the bible course, but one incident in particular remains in my mind.

I felt led one day to deviate from the main studies and refer to the Song of Solomon Chapter 1:6; *"Look not upon me, because I am black...."* In discussing this verse with the class, I soon learned how hurt and rejected they felt, because of comments made by certain white people about the colour of their skin.

It was my privilege to explain that as part of '*His church*' being the Bride of Christ, they were greatly loved and in no way, inferior to their white counterparts.

Zambia historical note:

Zambia, formerly Northern Rhodesia, received its name after independence in October 1964. The name Zambia was derived from The Zambezi river. Zambia is known for its three 'W's – Waterways, Wildlife and Witchcraft. The flag has a black area, recalling memories of once downtrodden people. Red is for the bloodshed to obtain freedom. Orange is for the copper belt. Ndola, where our missionaries operate, is part of the copper belt. On the flag, the green is for fertile land. The eagle, a native bird, signifies freedom and deliverance.

For the tourist, there are many attractions in Zambia including one of the seven natural wonders of the world, Victoria falls, which forms the watery border between Zambia and Zimbabwe.

Other features include the magnificent Lilac-coloured Jacaranda Trees; and the red 'bountiful' trees are a joy to behold.

Top - From left Pastor Roy Johnston (son-in-law) with Pastor Norman Christie in Zambia.
Bottom photo - Celebrating 50th Wedding Anniversay with family.
From left Philip, Pamela, Hilary, Sharon, Doreen & Pastor Norman Christie.

My return to Zambia...

Having had my first taste of Christian service in Zambia, I was keen to return as soon as possible.

However Pastor Roy was unable to return in 2019, but fortunately Mr Gary Moore, administrator with the L.I.F.T team, graciously allowed me to join the workers for their planned annual visit at the end of September.

This annual chosen date was selected to avoid the onset of the rainy season in November, which heralds the arrival of Malaria-carrying mosquitoes.

The. L.I.F.T vision is to carry out practical tasks in support of missionaries throughout the world. Coming from various denominations, they frequently and sacrificially forego their holidays, paying their own way in order to further the work of God. I was privileged to join their prayerful preparations in North Belfast. My Team was led by Mr Sandy Cranston who subsequently did an excellent job in leadership and practical work.

Scriptures which sustained me for this awesome adventure included; Isaiah 46:4; *"and even in your old age I am He; and even to hoar hairs will I carry you; I have made, and I will bear; even I will carry, and will deliver you."*

Further encouragement was taken from Isaiah 41:13; *"For I the LORD thy God will hold thy right hand, saying unto thee, Fear not; I will help thee."*

Medical preparations were made in Boots the chemist, who provided free of charge professional advice and Malaria tablets at very reasonable terms. Travel insurance was also necessary for such a lengthy trip.

In my case, being expected to do little practical work but much bible teaching, preparation for the events began months in advance. I was grateful for the preparation and advice from Mr Gary Moore, who arranged all our flights and drove the team to Dublin Airport for the take-off on Sunday 22, September 2019.

We flew to Addis Ababa via Madrid then to Ndola with Ethiopian Airways. Our well-balanced team consisted of Sandy Cranston, Elizabeth McClean, Colin Law, Anne Cobine and myself. Having left on Sunday, we arrived on Monday lunchtime, being scheduled to return by Monday October 7, 15 days later.

In addition to my sermon notes etc. I brought with me, 20 copies of Pastor Samuel T. Carson's book; *"Biblical times and seasons."*

However the 20 students of 2018 had become 36 students including Pastors and church leaders! This book became a text book for part of the course and was greatly appreciated by everyone.

Later in the year, I was able to send via Pastor Ziso a further batch of books to those who had not received.

On arrival we were delighted to learn that the 20 churches of 2018 were now 80 churches, well on the way to the vision of 100.

The next day we were examining the orphanage's huts to ascertain what was needed for maintenance, and then travelled to the site of a new Oasis church. This church would be led by its local pastor, namely Pastor Adam.

We returned to the orphanage and soon began the maintenance work, even though at times we had no electricity supply. One of the main needs was to replace the wire mesh which covered the windows to exclude the mosquitoes.

Unexpectedly on Thursday morning I was informed that classes would begin at 10am and was pleased to see about 30 students present. In Africa one has to be flexible.

On Friday we all travelled to the funeral of Pastor Stanley Ilunga at an old School room.

The grief of his family and African friends was very sad to behold, but yet in contrast, their tearful singing and worship was uplifting.

I returned to lectures, including a two-hour contribution from Andy Shadad, Elim's representative for the area. I was then advised that because of the bereavements there would be no more classes for four days.

Pastor Ziso was very much in need of a break, so on Monday afternoon he and I travelled by bus, a seven-hour journey to Lusaka, the capital of Zambia.

Following breakfast at 4am, we travelled to the Olga Hotel which was modern and well equipped.

We subsequently got a taxi to the five-star Royal Livingstone hotel, where we enjoyed a lovely afternoon tea and excellent facilities.

Ziso took many photographs of the nearby Zambezi river and the hotel grounds which included the animals.

We travelled to the Zambia side of Victoria falls and found that sadly, they were dry due to climate change. Late on Wednesday we went to see the Crocodile reptile park and took lots of photographs. It was all amazing especially when we were driven toward the nearby elephant herds. What an exciting break! We had joyfully witnessed the other side of life in Zambia.

On Thursday October 3, we left early for the 10-hour journey by bus to Lusaka, where we stayed overnight in an apartment. This time we managed to book flights on a new airline service using a Bombardier CRJ100 aircraft, arriving in Ndola at 7.30am.

My class of 36 students began receiving tuition at 9am.

We completed a prophecy class on the afternoon of Saturday October 5.

As always, it had been a pleasure to enjoy the hospitality and meals provided by Pastor Ziso and his wife Nicki.

For the orphans and everyone, it was great for the team to bring them all out to the café called, '*The Hungry Lion*' in Ndola, where we enjoyed ourselves immensely. But the best was yet to be!

The opening of Pastor Adams' new church on Sunday October 6, was just prior to our departure. It was a last minute change of plans and a total surprise. With the congregation assembled outside this new Ndola church I was given the great privilege of cutting the ribbon to let everyone in.

The joy and singing of the ladies and children's choirs were wonderful. After a few words of congratulations from Sandy and myself, we left the service early at 10:50am for our 1pm flight to Addis Ababa including a stop in Mozambique for 1.5 hours.

We then departed for our flight to Dublin at 7.55am on the Ethiopian Airways flight. There we were met by the faithful Gary Moore in the minibus and I was lucky to be the first one left home in Dromore.

Towards the end of that 2019 trip to Zambia, I had become increasingly aware that the mission pickup truck was unreliable. I decided to replace the 4x4 vehicle when I would return home. The roads of Zambia are either good, or sometimes atrocious such that only a 4x4 can survive for any length of time.

I thought it was going to take a long time to raise the necessary thousands of pounds, while also trusting God to answer prayer.

While attending one of the L.I.F.T prayer meetings, I was given the opportunity to mention this particular need.

A few poems were sold and the first small portion of funds were raised. However the Lord touched one man's heart to give a substantial amount of money towards this vehicle.

In a few days, I learned that he had contributed an amazing amount of £12,000. Our sales of the church printed poems came to about £450.

How delighted everyone was when within a few weeks of coming home, we were able to send the total amount to Zambia, resulting in a new vehicle being obtained very quickly. Not long afterwards, the Covid-19 pandemic occurred and all restrictions of lockdown were imposed. However the pastor of my Elim church in Donaghcloney was quick to develop online means of communication.

Meanwhile the local Presbyterian, Methodist, Church of Ireland and Elim churches had already combined in holding gospel services and prayer meetings in their churches.

Very fortunately the Presbyterian church had an ideal car park for drive-in services. These combined church services proved to be very successful and were held on Sunday afternoons during the lockdown. Through Pastor Phil Seifert's expertise, Donaghcloney Elim church began a broadly-based online outreach ministry. It was a privilege to take part in these presentations, including prayer meetings, bible studies etc. using Facebook with Zoom and Streamyard.

By these means, contact was made with folk living nearby and overseas. How exciting and thrilling it is to make oneself available for the King of Kings and the Lord of Lords!

To God be the Glory! May the Lord enable us all to prepare for life hereafter.

I present the following poem for your consideration...

Heavenly Bliss Above

In heavenly light abiding,
In joy beyond compare,
In love ever-increasing,
And Christ is everywhere.

What amazing consolation,
Transcending all our dreams.
Peace beyond imagination,
All wounds are healed, it seems.

Lost friends we loved surround us,
Our fellowship forever sweet,
Like little children full of glee,
We shall sit at His pierced feet.

All our hopes in Christ then realised,
His Glory fills the atmosphere,
Jesus there by all is worshipped,
Near Him, there shall be no fear.

Pastor Norman E Christie

CONTACT THE AUTHOR VISIT

Email
www.NormanChristie.com

INSPIRED TO WRITE A BOOK?

Contact
Maurice Wylie Media
Your Inspirational Christian Publisher

Based in Northern Ireland and distributing around the world.
www.MauriceWylieMedia.com